A Companion to
'THE ART OF FUGUE'

A Companion to
'THE ART OF FUGUE'
(*DIE KUNST DER FUGE*)
J. S. BACH

By

DONALD FRANCIS TOVEY
Sometime Reid Professor of Music in
the University of Edinburgh

MUSIC DEPARTMENT
OXFORD UNIVERSITY PRESS
LONDON   NEW   YORK   TORONTO

Oxford University Press
Music Department
44 Conduit Street, London, W.1

First published	*1931*
Second impression	*1951*
Third impression	*1960*
Fourth impression	*1966*
Fifth impression	*1970*

SBN: 19 323151 4

B ACH'S *Die Kunst der Fuge*, edited and
completed by Professor Tovey, is pub-
lished in a complete edition in open score for
the use of students by the Oxford University
Press.

A COMPANION TO BACH'S 'ART OF FUGUE'

THE student should make his own analysis of *Die Kunst der Fuge*; but his results will need verifying, and the following pages will serve his purpose.

Theorists are on solid ground when they tell us that the scheme of *Die Kunst der Fuge* (hereinafter called K. d. F.) involves some discrepancy between matter and form; but it is a mistake to assign this discrepancy to the technical difficulties Bach deals with. None of them are difficulties to him; with some of the apparently artificial schemes even the difficulties for ordinary mortals have been grossly overrated; and the first element of conflict comes where we least expect it—in the simplest fugues. For Bach uses the same subject in all; and a subject capable of the most elaborate stretti cannot be the kind of subject Bach would normally choose for a simple fugue. In *Das Wohltemperirte Klavier* (hereinafter called W. K.) the fugues that are as simple as Contrapunctus I and Contrapunctus II are the E major, Bk. I, No. 9; and in Bk. II the C major, No. 1; the E minor, No. 10; the F major, No. 11; the F minor, No. 12; the G major, No. 15; and the A major, No. 19. All the others have some such features as counter-subjects, identifiable recurring episodes, or stretti; and even the E minor and G major of Bk. II have rudimentary counter-subjects, while the recurring episodes in the F minor are very prominent. Now try to imagine any of these fugues with a serious subject!

One of the paradoxes of K. d. F. is that Bach found the making of simple fugues on a severe theme so interesting that he wrote no less than four without allowing himself any of the devices for which that theme was designed. These first four fugues are as remarkable a *tour de force* in composition as

the remaining fugues are in counterpoint. An elaborate
contrapuntal combination really greatly simplifies the composer's task. It is like those Japanese paper pellets which when
dropped into water unfold into flowers. The composer makes
the voices of his fugue announce the materials in separate
expositions, and then gradually combines them until he reaches
the final stage in which all the materials in combination go
through their most effective permutations and come to an end.
The actual art of composition in such a work lies in the
minutest details of its joints: the general scheme seems to
compose itself. But a simple fugue is almost a pure effort of
composition: it gives the composer no *a priori* guidance except
that its subject is passed from voice to voice, and that this
process is relieved by episodes arising naturally from the subject
and its accompaniments. Obviously the art of composition
here depends largely on the episodes; and if these are merely
connective tissue without strong recurring features, the composer's power of rhetoric is indeed severely tested. Such is the
No. I. problem Bach sets himself in Contrapunctus I. The subject

Ex. 1.

is announced by the alto. Upon its last note the soprano enters
with a *tonal* answer. The principle of tonal answer rests on the
fact that it is seldom desirable that each voice should crudely
transpose the subject into its own key. Accordingly a tonal
answer begins by lying *on* the dominant rather than *in* the
dominant. Or, in other words, the 5th from the tonic to
the dominant corresponds to the 4th from the dominant to
the tonic, and not to another 5th. A tonal answer shows its
character at the first convenient note, and afterwards proceeds
with the subject normally transposed, unless the subject
modulates to the dominant, in which case the answer must
contrive to return to the tonic. In the exposition (i.e. until all

the voices have entered with the subject) the only regular form
of answer is that which lies on or in the dominant, as

Ex. 2.

but, as the flat at the end of Ex. 2 shows, Bach does not allow
pedantries to interfere with his harmony. Many fine modu-
lations arise from 'irregular' later entries.

In the exposition of Contrapunctus I Bach has no gaps
between the entries of subject (S) and answer (A), and so the
first 16 bars consist of Alto, S; Soprano, A; Bass, S; and
Tenor, A. The counterpoint is not only simple but often of
a kind that hardly occurs away from keyboards. Often its
sense lies (like the quasi-counter-subject in the G major
Fugue, W. K. II, 15) rather in the combined result of the
rhythms ♩. ♪♩. ♪ and ♫♩ ♫♩ than in either of the
component parts. This kind of counterpoint continues, after
the exposition, from bar 17 to 24 while the alto rests. These
bars, then, are the first episode. In bar 24 the alto enters with
the subject. A merely interstitial episode separates this from an
entry of the subject in the soprano in bar 29. This is not an
answer, but a real transposition into the dominant, A minor.
It overlaps by one bar (32) a new kind of answer in the bass,
whereby the key swings round to G minor the subdominant.
The overlapping by one bar does not amount to a stretto; but
Bach had already in bar 29 been unable to resist a three-note
hint of a close stretto in the bass. It is very important with
Bach that we should never confuse such hints with his definite
contrapuntal devices. He always works his schemes out to the
last note as to completeness, however free he may be as to
variation. For instance, the theme of this fugue and of all the
others in the work, is always continued right to the first note
of its fifth bar. Again, a regular counter-subject is a highly
characteristic feature constantly accompanying the subject in

various positions. We must not give the name to the counterpoint of bars 6–8 in this first fugue merely because Bach does
not trouble to invent something different for the bass of bars
14–16.

At bar 36 another episode begins. It lasts only 4 bars, and
at bar 40 the tenor (after 5 bars rest) enters on the dominant
of D with another answer-form of the subject, landing it in
D minor. An episode 5 bars long leads to a similar entry in
the soprano, preceded by an anticipation of the first two notes
of the theme by the alto in bar 48. Three bars after the soprano
has finished the subject, the bass, having rested 6 bars, enters
in D minor (the soprano having, in bar 55, made another point
of a premonitory two notes). The bass carries the figure of the
4th bar down for three steps to the subdominant, from which
it moves to a dominant pedal. Meanwhile, with bar 60 the last
episode begins. It develops for 14 bars which end in an
emphatic close spaced out with rhetorical pauses. This close
ends on a tonic pedal over which, with subdominant tendency
and a major 3rd (*tierce de Picardie*), the tenor gives a final
answer-form of the subject, of which the last note (as usually
in K. d. F.) arrives with the last bar. The grandiose full close
in bars 70–4 is actually the only close in the whole fugue. The
last 5 bars are not in the 'Berlin autograph', which represents
Bach's first version, ending as follows:

It is evident that the important thing in this fugue is the way
in which it is spaced out. The uninterrupted exposition welds
the first 16 bars into a big symmetrical unit. The next 6 bars
of episode relieve the regularity. Then there is an entry of the

subject (which always accounts for 4 bars) with a gap of 2 bars between it and the next entry, which, however, in its turn overlaps the next by one bar. We thus have a series of three entries with a distinct effect of compression. Three other entries follow, each after a short (4 bar) episode, with a notice-able tendency to arouse anticipation in other parts; and at last we have a long episode of 14 bars making a climax and coming to the only (and therefore final) close in the composition. The counterpoint has given the composer no help whatever. Each entry of the subject is preceded by a rest, and each long rest is followed by an entry of the subject.

Contrapunctus II also has no definite contrapuntal device that can serve to shape the composition. But the counterpoint is given a strong character by means of dotting the fourth bar of the subject and deriving many sequences from its figure with the short notes boldly tied to the longer ones in systematic defiance of a common rule of rhythm in counterpoint. (See bar 5.) Where each part is played or sung by a separate person that rule is practical common sense; but in keyboard counter-point there is no awkwardness in playing the eccentric rhythm with some fingers and the accented beats with others. The exposition, in the order Bass, Tenor, Alto, Soprano (herein-after called **B, T, A, S**), again accounts for the first 16 bars without interruption: after which, 6 bars of episode end in a well-marked half-close on the dominant. Then in bar 23 **A**, imitated by the lower voices, appears to be starting another episodic figure in the dotted rhythm, but proves to have drifted into the subject, thus starting a counter-exposition in the order **A, S** (answer), **B** (after 1 bar), and **T** (after 3 bars). Two bars after **T** has finished, **S** enters high up with the subject in F major. (The rule about entries and rests is observed no longer in K. d. F. A part will often drift into the subject, and may enter with casual counterpoint after a long rest.) **A** answers **S** with a twist into G minor, immediately followed by **B** with a twist into B flat major. After 4 episodic bars **B**

enters again in D minor. Another 4-bar episode separates this
from an answer, syncopated, in **T**, after which 6 bars of episode
bring us to the final entry in **S**.

A point of great interest in the history of the work is that in
the Berlin autograph this fugue ended with a half-close, sub-

stituting the chord  for bar 78. This shows that

Bach at first had thoughts of playing some of the fugues in
sequence. It is unlikely that he ever thought of performing
the whole series at once: the very nature of the scheme is no
more favourable to good contrasts than the plan of a dictionary.
In the Berlin autograph this fugue is followed by Contrapunctus V. This fits the dominant close of II; and the
present IV, which also fits it, was not yet projected.

The composition of Contrapunctus II depends even more
than in Contrapunctus I on fine rhetorical detail. The student
can easily see the power of such detail by the effect *in situ* of
the return to D minor in bar 61. It would be very exciting to
achieve such a climax in an exercise.

No.
III.
Contrapunctus III is one of Bach's most beautiful pieces of
quiet chromatic slow music. (In the Berlin autograph it is
No. 2 and ends two bars earlier, at bar 70.) Counterpoint
emerges from the matrix of the keyboard style. The subject is
the inversion of Ex. 1—

Ex. 3.

and Bach begins with the tenor, in the position of an answer to
Ex. 3. In other words the subject of this fugue modulates at
once to the dominant and back, and has Ex. 3 for its answer.
The opening modulation has a mysterious effect which is
enhanced by the chromatic counterpoint which accompanies
the answer. This counterpoint, unlike the indeterminate
counterpoints of the previous fugues, is preserved as an

accompaniment to most of the later entries, and naturally occurs in the voice that last had the subject. It thus constitutes a regular counter-subject (hereinafter called c.-s.). An episode of 2 bars intervenes between the third entry (**S**) and the fourth (**B**). Theorists call an episode a *codetta* when it occurs before the end of the exposition. The distinction is not only useless but confusing when such an episode recurs later in the course of the fugue. Outside K. d. F. Bach seldom has an exposition unbroken by episode, and the 16-bar regularity of the first two fugues here is a special effect intended to give breadth to those otherwise restricted compositions.

The exposition of this third fugue, then, is in the order **T, A** (with counter-subject in **T**), **S** (c.-s. in **A**), and, after a 2-bar episode, **B** (c.-s. in **S**). A chromatic and sequential episode now follows; a 1-bar sequence in which the soprano and alto interchange parts at each step. This is a simple form of a device by which Bach in other highly organized fugues is able to make a straight sequence of many steps without monotony. In the present instance the bass never exchanges with the other parts; but similar episodes in other fugues are in triple counterpoint, with six possible positions (see the F sharp major fugue, W. K. II, 13). And the last episode in the 6-part fugue of *Das Musikalische Opfer* is in quadruple counterpoint, with 24 possible positions. It is important to realize the purpose of this device, viz. the grand simplicity of a long sequence underlying a constantly changing surface.

Call this passage (bars 19–22) the second episode. At bar 23, **S** (with c.-s. in **A**) gives an ornamental variation of the subject, with syncopations and passing-notes.

Ex. 4.

Such a device is unknown to the text-books, but is quite important in Bach's systems of fugue. You will find a very regular example carried through all four voices in close two-part stretti in the E major fugue, W. K. II, 9, bars 23–6. Here in Contrapunctus III Bach makes Ex. 4 an integral part of the fugue. After a 2-bar episode **T** has it in A minor (c.-s. again in **A**) and then again, after 2 bars, in F major (without c.-s.).

And now the composition begins to show symmetry by resuming Ep. 2 (bars 39–42). **S**, which has been resting for 12 bars, then enters with the plain subject in A minor (c.-s. in **A**). A new episode of 4 bars drifts into E♭ and C minor, from which point **B** (after 4 bars rest) moves into G minor with an entry of the plain subject. **A** replies in D minor with the variation Ex. 4 unsyncopated, entering a crotchet earlier (c.-s. in **T**). This overlaps by 1 bar with **S**, also in unsyncopated variation, and with a chromatic alteration in its last bar. After an interstitial bar the subject, unvaried, enters for the last time in **T**, and six more bars close the fugue. The Berlin autograph is two bars shorter, representing bar 70 by the following final chord:

No. Contrapunctus IV is later than the Berlin autograph. It is
IV. one of Bach's greater fugues and is a very lively study in episodes. They all arise from the quavers in the last bar of Ex. 3, direct and inverted, i.e. going up or going down, together with a cuckoo-like figure of a descending 3rd which is first represented by its characteristic iambic rhythm ♩ ♩ | ♩ ♩ ♩ in the counterpoints of the exposition, and which afterwards develops in ways easier to appreciate by ear than to describe.

The exposition is in the order **S, A** (with a characteristic

2-bar interlude), **T**, **B**. Episode 1 fills the 8 bars from 19 to 26. Then four entries follow without break; **S** in F, **A** in C, **T** in G minor, **B** (as answer) in D minor. Episode 2 begins by turning the parts of Ep. 1 round, the quavers being now in **S** and **A**, and the iambic 3rd in **T** and **B**, instead of vice versa. In 10 bars it comes (in A minor) to a full close (always a remarkable incident in a fugue) and proceeds on a new line for another 8 bars (53–60). Now comes a series of entries with what may be called an enhanced form of the subject. In a tonic position this splendid device would run thus, with the explanatory harmonies:

Ex. 5.

It has a powerfully rhetorical modulating effect. It first appears at bar 61 in **B**, starting in F and reaching G minor, where it is immediately answered by **T**, which thereby reaches the dominant of D. Four bars of episode intervene. The cuckoo-like 3rds, which have been making an insistent (though not fixed) counterpoint to the enhanced subject, now become rising 6ths. **A** enters with the enhanced subject in D minor moving to the dominant of A; and **S** follows in A minor going right over the dominant of E minor, a very bold venture. Episode 3 begins by inverting the treble of bars $45\frac{1}{2}$–$8\frac{1}{2}$ and swinging round to C major with a full close. Hereupon the lines of Ep. 1 are resumed and developed for another 16 bars closing in G minor (bar 103), after which the episode continues with the line taken in the latter part of Ep. 2 for 4 bars, having lasted 26 in all.

Bach is not allowing himself to use any of the contrapuntal devices for which his theme was designed; but he now gives it a treatment which is not exactly a stretto, but a kind of syncopated doubling in 3rds. At bar 107 **T**, in D minor, leads, doubled in syncopated lower 3rds by **B**. This combination is immediately answered by **S** and **A**. **S**, which is in the normal position for the answer, is syncopated, while **A** is on the beat a 6th below. The last episode begins at bar 115 on the prevalent lines of the scaly runs and the cuckoo-figure. But after 4 bars it proceeds to develop the beginning of Ep. 3, reinverting **S** of bars $45\frac{1}{2}$–$8\frac{1}{2}$ and 81–4 in **B** of bars 119–22, inverse answer in **A**. After 14 bars **T** enters in G minor with the enhanced subject, which closes into D minor, where a final entry in **A**, plus 2 bars, ends the fugue, over the usual tonic pedal.

A persistent repeated figure in bars 5 and 6 has often aided the cuckoo-figure in giving rhetorical force to the counter-point, but it does not amount to a steady counter-subject.

A word must be said about the tempo of these fugues. The time-signatures ¢ and C are no clue as Bach uses them, and in the present edition they are, with due warning in footnotes, altered according to their meaning in modern music. Nobody with a sense of beauty would want to take an alla-breve tempo for the lovely melancholy of Contrapunctus III; but anybody who thinks that in Contrapunctus IV such a passage as bars 53–60 could be slower than a fairly lively alla-breve must be in the state of mind imputed by Strachan-Davidson to the school-boy who 'believes in his heart that no nonsense is too enormous to be a possible translation of a classical author'.

No. We now come to the fugues for which the theme was de-
V. signed. Bach henceforth fills out the intervals as in Ex. 4 but without syncopation and without the graceful G before the B♭.

Contrapunctus V is a stretto-fugue in contrary motion. We may as well use the signs invented by Wesley and Horn for the first English edition of the W. K.: viz. ∧ for the normal subject, and ∨ for the inverted subject. With K. d. F. it will be convenient to take these signs in relation to the work as a whole. On this reckoning Contrapunctus V begins with ∨ in **A**, which is answered after 3 bars (instead of 4) by ∧ in **B**; whereupon, still at 3-bar intervals, **S** enters with ∧ answered by ∨ in **T**. A 3-bar episode, arising, as usual, from the quaver figure, leads to a counter-exposition at 3-bar intervals, in the order **S** ∨ (answer in A minor), **T** ∧ (A minor), **B** ∨ (D minor) **A** ∧. Another 3-bar episode leads to F major, where the stretti begin. Bach knows of no such rule as that the stretti should make their climaxes by appearing in gradually closer order. He does not think that climaxes depend on any such principle, and here he begins (in bar 33) at once with the closest stretto, **B** ∧; answered at half a bar by **S** ∨. Another 3-bar episode brings us to the converse stretto in G minor, **T** ∨; answered by **A** ∧. Another 2 bars (or 1½) takes us to B♭, where **B** and **T** give a new stretto in the octave at a bar and a half, both parts with ∨. And now comes an episode on the figure of bar 1 in close 4-part canon (at crotchet distances) on the first figure of ∨. Bach would certainly not call this a stretto, but a mere imitative episode; though it is exactly like the passages in Handel's Amen chorus, on the strength of which Rockstro tells us that that most improvisatory of fugues is a marvel of close stretto. Bach makes 4 bars of this episode lead to the inversion of the second stretto, **S** ∧ in D minor, answered at 1½ bars an octave lower by **A** ∧. (The soprano entry shows, like the tenor entry in bar 41, how Bach uses the idea of a tonal answer to swing from one key to another by substituting a 4th for the initial 5th. The student should note other cases for himself. This is one of the simple subtleties by which fugues I and II are kept alive without further apparatus.)

Another interstitial episode now leads in 3 bars to an inversion of the 4-part canonic passage that forms the only characterized episode in this fugue. In bars 65–8 the figure of ∧ is thus worked into canon at crotchet distances. The parts are not in the exact reverse order of bars 53–6, though they could have been so arranged. But such 'mirror' inversions belong to a later problem. This episode leads back to D minor, where we have a third plan of stretto, in the 8ve at 1 bar. (This requires accessory parts to support the 4ths which come on the beat in the only possible position. Other positions would result in consecutive 5ths.) First, bars 69–72 show **S** ∨ answered by **T** ∨. The usual 3 bars of interstitial episode intervene before we come to the converse stretto, **T** ∨ answered by **A** ∧. The bass should normally have led here, but Bach (who never lets machinery interfere with good music) is reserving it for the final entry, which follows after a 4-bar episode. This makes an emphatic close into a final tonic pedal over which, with a major *tierce de Picardie*, the voices break into 6 parts and the alto with the upper bass give the direct and inverted themes simultaneously; ⋀⋁. Great rhetorical power is not to be expected from this fugue. Its stretti are all extraordinarily smooth, and not (in Bach's estimation) very different from each other. The structure is punctuated by the half-closes at bars 52 and 64 before those imitative episodes which are the backbone of the composition. Otherwise, smoothness is the main point of the whole. Bach has made incalculable progress since the early stretto-fugues in D♯ minor and A minor which he admitted into Bk. I of W. K. Such crudenesses as the following, from the D♯ minor fugue—

Ex. 6.

would be wholly inadmissible in K. d. F., though the alto in the fifth bar of Ex. 6 would certainly sound more convincing if it could have been played without skipping to the higher 8ve. But playability is as strict a condition in K. d. F. as in W. K.

No. VI.   Contrapunctus VI is a solid mass of stretto with the subject not only direct and inverted but also diminished in both forms. Wesley and Horn use the sign ⃞ for diminution, and we must combine it with the other signs. Thus the exposition brings in three parts within 3 bars; **B** ∧, **S** ⇓, **A** ⇑. Two bars after **B** has finished its full-sized subject **T** enters with ⇓. The episodes are mere interstitial though they make excellent use of the first figure of the diminished subject. For the rest the fugue is uninterrupted stretto; and when the student has amused himself by putting the above signs into the score (being scrupulous in not so labelling mere fragments) he has analysed nearly all that is meant to be studied. He can penetrate into details by labelling the first 4 or 6 notes of the subject '(a)' and the last 5 notes (the final turn) '(b)'; and this will enable him to see that the episodes and interstitial counterpoints are not without organization. He may label the short demisemiquaver runs (in the style of a French overture) with the letter x if he agrees with me that Bach is not intending to derive them from (b).

I do not recommend a solemn attitude towards these three stretto fugues V, VI, and VII. Yet it is impossible to overrate the mastery shown in their perfect smoothness. And to make reasonably effective compositions out of such uniform masses of stretto is almost as great a *tour de force* as to make them, like fugues I and II, with no fugue-devices at all. On the whole Nos. VI and VII are aesthetically about as important as No. I, which No. VI resembles in the feature of reserving its one full close for the final climax. (You must not call every tonic chord a full close when it is preceded by a dominant: that incident in bars 11–12 does not stop the flow.)

Nothing is more overrated than the difficulty of making contrapuntal combinations. There is no difficulty: your combinations will work automatically if they are going to work at all. An experienced composer acquires an instinct for combinations that work. An inexperienced composer, if he is conscientious, says to preconceived materials '*Marche, ou je t'assomme*', and, like Adam de la Hale, rough-hews the main accents into concord. If he is one of our noble liberators from classical prejudice, he simply says '*Ça marche*' over any number of things he chooses to put together, and thunders his anathemas at any critic so blasphemous as to object. All the ingenuity of K. d. F., except a few freakish fireworks, was settled once for all when Bach invented first that wonderfully plastic subject and, secondly-to-seventhly, certain other subjects that combine with it. At present he is engaged in the comparatively trivial task of combining it with itself; and he is unable to pile up his stretti to noble climaxes like those of the stretto fugues in W. K. I, C major and W. K. II, D major, simply because there are too many of them here. These fugues are restricted not by their ingenuity but by what is for Bach their ridiculous ease.

No. VII. Contrapunctus VII adds augmentation to the diminution, and has no episodes at all except bars 32–4. Its composition must have been a very simple process, after Bach had collected his material for the whole K. d. F. to begin with. He probably first wrote the 4 bars which lead to the entry of the bass with the augmented inverted subject. (Wesley and Horn use the sign ⌐ for augmentation.) Then he wrote out the bass in the following 8 bars, properly spaced to leave room for 16 notes to a bar. He then put whatever entries and counterpoints came handy above this: including the double-diminution of (a).

Ex. 7.

Of course the diminished subject can slip in some two or three times while ▽ is booming in the bass. This takes us to bar 14. Bach probably blocked out the rest of the fugue in the same way from each augmentation to the next. From bar 14 he proceeds with the ordinary and diminished subject for 9 bars. Note the running catch-up in the course of V in **A,** and also the fact that Bach does not mind giving ⋀ twice in the same position to **T,** with only one intervening bar. (This is an extreme case of Bach's deliberate contempt for a rule about which some eighteenth-century theorists were very strict. The

student should note other cases for himself, and should not
fail to observe how all suspicion of tautology disappears in the
general result. Bach never uses a rule as a substitute for his
own judgement. This particular rule is as powerless to avoid
tautology as a rule for calling Bach 'the Leipzig Cantor' and
'the master-contrapuntist', &c., &c., in alternate sentences.)

At bar 23, **T** runs into △ in F major, and this settles the
business of the next 8 bars. After the only episode of 3-bars'
length, **A** enters in D minor with ▽ against the $1\frac{1}{2}$-bar stretto
of ∧ at the 8ve. Then 7 bars of the diminished subject lead to
△ high up in **S** by way of climax. Four final bars come to the
close. There are no other closes.

The C major organ fugue

Ex. 8.

shows how such a stretto-scheme can be given a grand
rhetorical effect. It reserves the augmentation for a long-
delayed first entry of the pedals, to which the augmentation is
confined, and which devote themselves to it exclusively. Such
a device was not open to Bach in the scheme of K. d. F.; but
I found myself driven to use its aesthetic equivalent in my
conjectural finish of the great quadruple fugue.

Now we come to the central business of K. d. F.; the fugues No.
in double and triple counterpoint, or fugues in which the VIII.
motto-theme is combined with others. Such fugues are those
which Bach most enjoys working out on a large scale, and there
is nothing in the scheme of K. d. F. to prevent them from
being pure works of art. Accordingly these examples are
among his greatest compositions and must be taken on their
individual merits.

Contrapunctus VIII is a triple fugue with three strongly
contrasted subjects. And here it is well to call attention to
the real nature and purpose of polyphony. Much vexatious

damage is done to the enjoyment of music, even for musicians
themselves, by the mistaken notion that in order to understand
polyphony you must be able to attend to all the parts at once.
No such mistake was made by the sixteenth-century theorists
to whom Palestrina's polyphony was the final outcome of a tradition as ancient to them as Bach is to us now. They analysed
their harmony as between two parts at a time; and this was
adequate. For every fault of harmony exists between two parts;
and if it at the same time concerns more, we can call it more
than one fault. If in the 6-part polyphony of the *Missa Papae
Marcelli* or the 40-part polyphony of Tallis's *Spem in alium*
there are no faults, then our enjoyment of the euphony does
not depend on our attending to the individual parts. It is the
same with combinations of themes: a piece of triple counterpoint is, or ought to be, a satisfactory mass of harmony in the
first place. Secondly, this harmony happens to be produced
by three pregnant melodies so disposed that any can be a bass
or treble to the others. Consequently this mass of harmony
can be presented in six positions, every one of which has a
different surface or bass. To complain that we cannot attend
to all three themes at once is like arguing that no picture ought
to be larger than a postage-stamp because that is fully as large
an area as the eye's centre of clear vision can comprise.

   In point of fact, Bach's triple counterpoints (like the *coup
d'œil* of a big picture) produce an immediate effect before we
make any effort of attention. The themes are so contrasted
as to be transparent to each other. One will trickle along in a
rapid movement which would be audible even in an undertone
against the others. Another will have wide skips which will
always attract attention even in an inner part. The third will
perhaps consist of some long notes in a chain of suspended
discords; which is as much as to say that it provides the main
harmonic effect. Or it may have some peculiar rhythm. See
the combinations of a subject with two counter-subjects in
W. K. I, C mi., C♯ ma., B♭ ma.

Contrapunctus VIII is on the lines of W. K. I, C♯ mi. and II, F♯ mi.; in which three subjects are given equal prominence by being introduced in separate sections, their complete combination being reserved for a later stage. (In the great C♯ minor fugue the third subject soon joins the second in making triple counterpoint with the first; and the final stage is devoted to piles of stretto on $\wedge_1 + \wedge_3$.)

The composer's first task in such a fugue is to make his final combination. The listener will understand the aesthetic values of the work much better if he regards this combination as a single idea than if he persists in trying to keep its threads separate; in other words, than if he refuses to follow the composer's intention of pulling the whole together.

Here, then, is the 'idea' of Contrapunctus VIII:

Ex. 9.

Like all good triple and multiple counterpoints these three neither begin together nor end together. They are perfectly transparent to each other. The quickly-moving $\wedge_2$ makes suspended discords with $\wedge_1$. And $\wedge_3$, which is the inverted motto-theme of K. d. F., is conspicuous by its broken rhythm, a delightful instance of Bach's power of variation, and very suggestive of Brahms.

Three such themes are enough for a very big fugue; and so this is one of Bach's biggest. The first section is a broad exposition of the topmost theme of Ex. 9, led off by **A**. The gap of $1\frac{1}{2}$ bars between the very first voice and its answer is rare in Bach: it here has the effect of prolonging the subject, as all three parts at first use the figure it contains. The rest of the counterpoint does not form a regular counter-subject, but its figures are used constantly. You may, if you like, derive the figure of bars 7–8 by diminution from bars 5–6, though I doubt whether this is Bach's way of thinking. At all events, if you letter the figure as (x), and the first notes of bar 9 as (y), you will then be able to account for most of the quaver counterpoints as made of x+y direct and inverted.

Ex. 10.

Ex. 11.

Six bars after the exposition **A** has an entry of $\underset{1}{\wedge}$ in A minor with a suggestion of close stretto in **B**. But stretto is not the business of this fugue, and imitative suggestions are all that appear in it. A sequence is developed from the main figure of $\underset{1}{\wedge}$ in bars 28–30, and at bar 35 **B** concludes the first section with the whole theme, ending at bar 39.

Now, as in the great C♯ minor fugue, $\underset{2}{\wedge}$ makes its first appearance already in combination with $\underset{1}{\wedge}$. It is in **A**, below $\underset{1}{\wedge}$ in **S**. Before answering $\underset{1}{\wedge}$ **B** throws in a new figure $(\underset{z}{\wedge})$ (not to be confused with the x y groups) in G minor.

Ex. 12.

It then proceeds with $\underset{1}{\wedge}$ in that key, **S** having $\underset{2}{\wedge}$. After an interval of 2 bars from the end of this, we have a third entry in A minor (**A** $\underset{1}{\wedge}$, **B** $\underset{2}{\wedge}$). Then there is a 7-bar episode developing $\underset{z}{\wedge}$ and $\underset{v}{z}$. At bar 61 we have **S** $\underset{1}{\wedge}$ with **A** $\underset{2}{\wedge}$ in F major, followed, after a 2-bar interlude at **B** $\underset{1}{\wedge}$ with **S** $\underset{2}{\wedge}$ in B flat, making a close. The next episode begins with the $\underset{z}{\wedge}+\overset{z}{\vee}$ development, but at bar 74 it takes up the figure of $\underset{2}{\wedge}$, which is in any case a sequence that can be prolonged indefinitely, so that no line can be drawn between the fixed theme and its episodic developments. This gives a subtle and perhaps intentional point to casual resemblances to $\underset{1}{\wedge}$ (with reversed accents) in bars 74–6. An unmistakable but unfinished entry of $\underset{1}{\wedge}$ comes in **A** at the end of bar 79; **B** having already begun to unroll the figure of $\underset{2}{\wedge}$. After two bars **S** takes the point up with a complete D minor entry of $\wedge$ over $\underset{2}{\wedge}$ in **A**; and the following episode brings this second section to an end with a climax. Beginning with the $\underset{z}{\wedge}+\overset{z}{\vee}$ matter, it treats the figure of $\underset{2}{\wedge}$ in close imitation while **B** alludes to $\underset{1}{\wedge}$; and then the episode comes with a flourish (implying a big *rallentando*) to a half-close (bar 93).

$\underset{z}{\wedge}$ in **B** (followed by the long-forgotten x) answered by $\overset{z}{\vee}$ in **S** (which continues with $\underset{y}{\wedge}$), form free counterpoints to $\underset{3}{\wedge}$; our K. d. F. theme inverted, with a charming new broken rhythm. The figure of $\underset{0}{\wedge}$ (but not the whole theme) also joins the counterpoints. After a bar's interlude **B** gives the answer of $\underset{3}{\wedge}$; and after a 2-bar interlude **S** has it, also in A minor. The next episode develops $\underset{y}{\wedge}$ and $\overset{y}{\vee}$ for 5 bars and then suddenly plunges into what sounds like $\underset{2}{\wedge}$ over $\underset{1}{\wedge}$ on a tonic pedal D. But this turns out to be only a sequence, which starts the episode on a new imitative development of the figure of $\underset{2}{\wedge}$. This leads to a close in A minor. The figure of $\underset{2}{\wedge}$ is resumed in **B** and answered by the whole theme $\underset{2}{\wedge}$ in **S** in an abnormal relation to $\underset{1}{\wedge}$ which appears in **A**, partially but effectively doubled in 3rds by **B**. (The abnormality in this relation of $\underset{2}{\wedge}$ to $\underset{1}{\wedge}$ consists in the fact that it is not only at a different pitch, which in itself would mean inversion in a double counterpoint other than in the 8ve, but that it combines at a different point, a device for which the books have no name.)

The old extra bars (5 and 6) reappear. **B** answers, with $\hat{2}$ in **A** at the normal point and pitch. Then a 12-bar episode on $\hat{z}$ and $\overset{z}{\vee}$ leads to the stage for which this fugue has been preparing for 146 bars. With bar 147 the triple counterpoint begins. According to the position of the themes it should be in F major, but a bold handling of accidentals (unknown in principle to text-books) warps the first 3 bars into A minor, and very boldly warps the answer into E minor. Only the third entry is normal to its key of G minor. These entries, with the whole last section of the fugue, are best tabulated as follows:

Bars 147–51 $\left\{\begin{array}{l}\hat{1}\\\hat{2}\\\hat{3}\end{array}\right.$ F (disguised as A mi.)

Bars 152–6 $\left\{\begin{array}{l}\hat{3}\\\hat{1}\\\hat{2}\end{array}\right.$ C (disguised as E mi.)

2 bars ($1\frac{1}{2}$) interlude

Bars 158 (end)–63 $\left\{\begin{array}{l}\hat{2}\\\hat{3}\\\hat{1}\end{array}\right.$ G mi.

7 bars episode on new lines, ending with figure of $\hat{2}$.

Bars 170–5 $\left\{\begin{array}{l}\hat{3}\\\hat{2}\\\hat{1}\end{array}\right.$ D mi.

8 bars episode on lines of the previous one.

Bar 182 (end) to end of fugue $\left\{\begin{array}{l}\hat{1}\\\hat{2}\\\hat{3}\end{array}\right.$

Contrapunctus IX is in double counterpoint (hereinafter called D-C) at the 12th. The object of this device is to obtain two different harmonic schemes from one pair of melodies. Ordinary interchange of parts by an octave or two does not alter the roots of the harmony; but a properly managed D-C in 12th produces two markedly different harmonic effects besides changing the expression of the shifted theme. The concord of the 6th inverts into a 7th, and the shifted theme assumes a new colouring of dominant or subdominant according to circumstances.

In the Berlin autograph this fugue is No. 5, which shows only that it probably occurred to Bach before others which should precede it. But its notation gives the K. d. F. theme in its normal time, and so we may use it in the following paradigm:

Ex. 13.

In 12th.

Original position.

The shifting tonality of the running theme when it is placed a 12th higher is very interesting and, as the alternative accidentals show, capable of some free play.

Bach, feeling that the semiquavers might suggest too quick

a tempo, changed the notation, doubling the note-values and halving the bars. We should, however, misinterpret him if we took his new ₵ time-signature to mean 4 in a bar: it must be sufficiently like *alla breve* to account for his ever having thought of semiquavers at all. But not too fast for the details of bars 20–1. I cannot account for the manifest perversity of Bach's use and non-use of the *alla-breve* time-signatures. But the choice of note-values is another matter with method in it. A notation in quavers and semiquavers has its advantages in keyboard polyphony; for the quaver-bars often show the continuity of a part that moves from one stave to the other, whereas crotchets and minims show no connexion. In open score this advantage disappears; and the engraver (whose point of view Bach thoroughly understood) merely has some 30 per cent. more work with those troublesome heavy lines. Moreover, the open score, with its four vocal clefs, is associated with choral music, and Bach accordingly changed to the characteristic choral note-values when he decided to put the work into score. It is a melancholy reflection that if the Berlin autograph had remained our only text of K. d. F. we should have suffered from no nonsense as to its not being practical keyboard music, and should not even have been led to lay more stress on its theoretical aspect than is implied by its title and its use of one theme throughout all its numbers.

Bach changed his notation in similar ways elsewhere; e.g. in the A major organ-fugue, and in the 48th prelude of W. K. In later music there is the interesting case of Mendelssohn re-writing the *alla-breve* bars of the *Midsummer Night's Dream* overture as common-time bars of twice the length in his pianoforte arrangement; and Wagner, in Isolde's *Liebestod*, transcribes 100 *alla-breve* bars of the duet in the 2nd Act as 50 common-time bars.

Contrapunctus IX begins with an uninterrupted exposition of its running theme (which we will call $\wedge_1$), in the order **A, B, S, T.** A 6-bar episode (the student can letter its figures already in the running theme) leads to the entry of $\wedge_2$ in **S** with $\wedge_1$ in **T**. This is followed (with only a 2-bar interlude) by the inversion in the 12th in F major, $\wedge_2$ in **T**, $\wedge_1$ at 12th in **A**. Another 6-bar episode returns to D minor, where we have the original combination, $\wedge_2$ in **A**, $\wedge_1$ in **B**. Again a 6-bar episode leads to A minor, where the inversion in the 12th is again given to **A** and **T**. The next episode takes 8 bars, and, as in Contrapunctus I, hints of the K. d. F. theme are given by premonitory rising 5ths or 4ths. At bar 89 the twelfth-position appears, $\wedge_2$ in **B** with $\wedge_1$ at 12th in **S**. This is immediately followed (with only 1 bar's interlude) with the same thing in G minor between **T** and **A**, who have thus had it 3 times out of 4. Then follows the last episode, 12 bars long, which leads to the final entry of the original combination, $\wedge_2$ in **A** and $\wedge_1$ in **T**, and so to the end of a very brilliant and straightforward fugue.

Contrapunctus X is in D-C at the 10th. The mere inversions at this interval have no distinct character; but they have the advantage that they can be used with the original position simultaneously. Consequently they make it possible to double either or both of the melodies in 3rds or 6ths. Perhaps the three finest examples in the world are this fugue, the G minor fugue in W. K. II (which is also in the 12th and makes magnificent use of the turning of 6ths into 7ths), and the *Pleni sunt coeli* of the B minor Mass, where in one of the positions the main theme is in the bass doubled three 8ves and a 3rd higher by a trumpet, while the other theme is in close 3rds for inner voices.

Bach originally began Contrapunctus X at bar 23 with **S** alone as a normal fugue-opening, with the answer in **T** as at bar 26. This early version was mistakenly included in the original edition and most others. Even Rust, in the Bachgesellschaft edition, could not resolve to remove it to the appendix. There is really no reason why it should be printed at all; the purposes of the most exhaustive edition would be served by

No.
X.

a list of its trivial differences from the final version, apart from
what has just been said.

The page which Bach added to the beginning is one of the
profoundest and most beautiful he ever wrote. The broken
rhythm and varied tonality of the new theme, with its wistful
run up to C♮, give an effect of poetic mystery deepened by the
peculiar structure of the exposition. To begin with, Bach
breaks an old rule which he was never concerned to keep, but
which the main theme of K. d. F. keeps for him, the rule that
the first note of a fugue must be either the tonic or the dominant. But now his new theme, announced by **A**, begins with
the leading-note; and the answer by **T** is in the subdominant,
breaking the rule that allows only the dominant as a modulation
during the exposition. (In W. K. the fourth entry of the great
C♯ minor fugue breaks this rule, and so does the subject,
already beginning on the leading-note, of the F♯ major fugue
in Bk. II.)

Then **B** inverts the subject and is answered in stretto at
1½ bars by **S**. After an interlude of 2½ bars there is another
very close stretto at the half-bar between ∧ in **A** (with an
impressive subsidence from A minor to G minor) and ∨ in **T**,
5 more bars bring the section to a half-close (bar 22). **S** then
enters with ∧, which is the inverted K. d. F. theme as in
Contrapunctus V. **A** answers in partial stretto at 1 bar in the
4th (apparently the 5th, to the first note, but it is a tonal
answer). This stretto has not occurred before in K. d. F.,
because it cannot be carried through; but it makes its point
here. In due course **T** answers, and the accessory voices rest.
The figure in bar 28

Ex. 14.

does not form a regular counter-subject, but is afterwards
given extraordinary prominence in episodes. (This fugue ranks

with No. 4 as one of Bach's greatest examples of episodic development.)

In the exposition of $\bigwedge_{2}$ as it ran in the first draft, i.e. without the accessory **A** and **B** of bars 23–6, the voices expose $\bigwedge_{2}$ without break and always at 3-bar distances (as in No. 5), in the order **S, T, B, A.**

After a 6-bar episode the first combination of $\begin{cases} \bigwedge_{2} \\ \bigwedge_{1} \end{cases}$ appears in **A** and **T** (bars 44–8). An interlude of 4 bars (introducing x in **S**) leads to the inversion in the 10th, $\begin{cases} \mathbf{A} \bigwedge_{1} \\ \mathbf{B} \bigwedge_{2} \end{cases}$ in 10th.

The following paradigm shows how the position at the 10th can be used together with the original model:

Ex. 15.

Such a scheme has any number of permutations; far more than the twenty-four of a genuine quadruple counterpoint. Either or both themes may be doubled in 3rds either above or below, or in 6ths above or below, or, as here, in 10ths with one part in the middle. And the two themes are very likely to be invertible in the 12th as well as in the 10th. This is the case here and also in the great G minor fugue of W. K. II, where Bach doubles both themes at once. The present combination would be in too stiff a rhythm without keeping one part free to move in its own way. For this and other reasons not a quarter of even the typical permutations are used, to say nothing of the stretti.

Bars 56–65 are an episode which takes the unorthodox form

of a series of three entries of x, with much of the effect of a fugal exposition of a new subject. Then, in bars 66–70 we have the inversion in the 10th, $\begin{cases} \mathbf{S} \; \wedge_1 \\ \mathbf{B} \; \wedge_2 \end{cases}$ in 10th.

A 5-bar episode on the last quavers of $\wedge_2$ leads to the combination $\wedge_1$ doubled in lower 6ths in **S**, **A**, over $\wedge_1$ in **B**. The resulting key is F major. The next episode develops a new figure, (y),

Ex. 16.

for 6 bars. Then, swinging from G minor to D minor we have the combination $\wedge_2$ doubled in 3rds over $\wedge_1$, with the following result:

$$\begin{cases} \mathbf{S} \; \wedge_1 \text{ in 12th} \\ \mathbf{A} \; \wedge_1 \text{ in 10th} \\ \mathbf{B} \; \wedge_2 \end{cases}$$

The next episode again introduces a new figure $\wedge_z$, with $\vee_z$. This should be viewed as a whole; its character is independent of its optical resemblance to an ornamented figure of $\wedge_1$.

Ex. 17.

Yet a new imitative scale-figure appears in bars 98–100. After a total length of 14 bars this episode reaches B♭ major, where (bars 103–6) we have the combination

$$\begin{cases} \mathbf{S} \; \wedge_2 \\ \mathbf{T} \; \wedge_1 \text{ upper 3rd} \\ \mathbf{B} \; \wedge_1 \end{cases}$$

The last episode fills the 8 bars 107–14. Re-establishing (and taking only 4 bars to re-establish) D minor, it leads to the final combination—

$$\begin{cases} \mathbf{A} \underset{1}{\wedge} \text{ in 12th} \\ \mathbf{T} \underset{1}{\wedge} \text{ in 10th} \\ \mathbf{B} \underset{2}{\wedge} \end{cases}$$

with which the fugue ends almost abruptly. It is a wonderful study in an almost modal mixture of tonality. Played quietly throughout, its effect is as romantic as anything in Bach. Notice that the harmonic character is not only deliberately sought, but is brought about mainly by the D-C in the 10th. This is perhaps the only case where a definite harmonic effect has ever been obtained from inversion in the 10th apart from its use in added 3rds.

In Contrapunctus XI Bach sets himself to work out a triple No. fugue on the inversion of the three subjects of Contrapunctus XI. VIII. The Berlin autograph puts it immediately after that fugue; an arrangement which has its point. The notation of both fugues in 2/4 time, with notes of half the present values, is another interesting indication of tempo, the inference being that Bach was afraid of taking these fugues too fast. No. XI is the most difficult of all the aesthetically important parts of K. d. F., and is the better for a tempo appreciably slower than that of No. VIII.

The task Bach here sets himself is not strictly possible. Of the three themes the motto-theme is the only one that was naturally conceived as invertible. The first theme of VIII can still be construed when inverted, but is then obviously not a spontaneous idea. The second theme makes a series of suspensions that when inverted will resolve ungrammatically upwards instead of downwards. Bach, instead of attempting to construe the resulting harshness, avoids all difficulty by representing the inversion of $\underset{2}{\wedge}$ by a similar theme which indeed climbs up instead of down, but which resolves its discords respectably.

The student may make his own choice of a convention for the analytic signs of this fugue. I find it best to abandon all attempt to make the signs run through the whole of K. d. F.

and I prefer to treat this fugue as an independent work, acknowledging the whole scheme only by once putting a star to the motto-theme.

We will accordingly disregard No. VIII and will mark the opening theme of No. XI as Λ_1. It is given an unbroken exposition in the order **A, S, T, B**. Note that Bach does not spoil his answer by trying to make it tonal. That could be done either by making it go into the subdominant, or by stumbling over two D's in the first bar. Common sense forbids such pedantries. The last bar of the theme gives rise to a 4-bar episode, after which **S** drifts once more into the subject, with crowded imitations in the other parts. This concludes the first section with a full close.

Now **A** gives out Λ_2, an inversion of the Λ_1 in Contrapunctus VIII. Bach, not being proud of the melodic result of this inversion, conceals it beneath a rising chromatic scale, which we will call Λ_x. This figure never rounds itself off as a definite subject; but, with its inversion (promptly appearing in **B**), it henceforth pervades the fugue and makes it typically chromatic. With Bach this kind of chromatic texture is one of the recognized species of fugue. He had already used it in No. III: its presence in Frederick the Great's theme impels the fugues in *Das Musikalische Opfer* to fall into the same style, and it may be recognized locally in the pair of new counter-subjects in the second stretto of the great E major fugue, W. K. II, bars 16–21.

At great leisure Bach makes his exposition of this chromatic combination, which is harmonically gorgeous. Three bars elapse before **T** answers; and an episode of one-bar steps in triple counterpoint (Ep. 2) rotates for 6 bars before **B** has its turn. Then a 9-bar episode (Ep. 3) follows, on new lines (Ep. 2), at last drifting into the steps of Ep. 1. Then (bars $55\frac{1}{2}$–60) **S** enters with Λ_2, but re-inverted into its rightful shape as in No. VIII. This shows how sensitive Bach is to aesthetic values in this fugue: he will not allow the grotesque inversion to appear more prominently than he can help.

Episode 4 carries on the permutations of Ep. 2 for 8 bars, after which $\underset{2}{\vee}$ (i.e. the right form of No. VIII $\underset{1}{\wedge}$) enters in the bass and brings this section to a full close in A minor.

The third section consists of a regular exposition of $\underset{1}{\vee}$ ($= \underset{3}{\wedge}$ of No. VIII and $\vee$ of K. d. F.). The order is **T** (A minor), **S** (D mi.), **B** (answer), **A** (D mi.). Two bars, added to these regular 16, make the third formal close in F.

The fourth section introduces $\underset{3}{\wedge}$ of this fugue in combination with $\underset{2}{\wedge}$. As we have seen, $\underset{3}{\wedge}$ cannot, for harmonic reasons, be a true inversion of $\underset{2}{\wedge}$ in No. VIII. In its present form it is a figure that can rise indefinitely and be doubled in 3rds and 6ths. Both **T** and **A** take advantage of this, while $\underset{2}{\wedge}$ (or $\underset{3}{\vee}$ of No. VIII) rises in the deep bass. (Some commentators see in the alto of bar 91 an allusion to Bach's name. I cannot believe either that Bach would first have anticipated this by the tenor in another key, or that he spelt his name Baccch.) **A** and **S** answer the two themes in bars $94\frac{1}{2}$–7; after which **S** imitates an episode on the rightful form of the figure of $\underset{3}{\wedge}$ (as in $\underset{u}{\wedge}$ of No. VIII). This (Ep. 5) lasts only for 4 bars, after which $\underset{1}{\wedge}$ (accompanied by the 'rightful' quaver theme) enters in **A** in D minor. It is immediately followed by a new combination:

$$\left\{ \begin{array}{l} \mathbf{A} \overset{3}{\vee} (= \underset{2}{\wedge} \text{ of VIII}) \\ \mathbf{T} \overset{2}{\vee} (= \underset{1}{\wedge} \text{ of VIII}) \\ \mathbf{B} \overset{x}{\vee} \end{array} \right.$$

The harmony is turned aside into B♭; and a sixth episode develops for 5 bars on the lines of Ep. 5, closing into the combination $\left\{ \begin{array}{l} \mathbf{S} \underset{1}{\wedge} \\ \mathbf{A} \underset{2}{\wedge} \end{array} \right.$ with $\underset{x}{\wedge}$ in the bass. Episode 7 develops both versions of $\underset{3}{\wedge}$ together with $\underset{x}{\wedge}$ and $\overset{x}{\vee}$ with great vigour for 15 bars, coming at the twelfth bar to the fourth formal close in this fugue. From this close in A minor the remaining 3 bars return to D minor with the quaver figures rising in 6ths in a true inversion over the descending figure in 3rds. Now (bars 133–6) **B** gives $\underset{1}{\wedge}$ while **S** and **A** in 6ths have $\underset{2}{\vee}$ inverted (i.e. the figure of $\underset{2}{\wedge}$ in No. VIII). Then **T**, instead of answering **B**, enters with $\underset{2}{\wedge}$ while **S** and **A** in 3rds have $\underset{3}{\wedge}$. Episode 8 continues the line of Ep. 7 for 6 bars, closing into C major. This turns off into E minor, where we now have the combination of the three themes intended to represent the inversion of the combination in No. VIII. In bars 146–9 the order is

$$\left\{ \begin{array}{l} \mathbf{S}\ \underset{2}{\wedge} \\ \mathbf{A}\ \underset{3}{\wedge} \\ \mathbf{T}\ \underset{1}{\wedge} \end{array} \right.$$

in E minor. Episode 9 continues on the lines of Ep. 7. But now, instead of answering the triple counterpoint, Bach takes a new line and shows us the simultaneous combination of $\underset{1}{\wedge}$ and $\underset{1}{\vee}$ that had appeared at the end of Contrapunctus V. Bars 158–62 show the position $\left\{ \begin{array}{l} \mathbf{S}\ \overset{1}{\vee} \\ \mathbf{A}\ \underset{1}{\wedge} \end{array} \right.$. After a 2-bar interlude this is answered in G minor by $\left\{ \begin{array}{l} \mathbf{T}\overset{1}{\underset{1}{\wedge}} \\ \mathbf{B}\ \vee \end{array} \right.$, inverted in D-C at the 10th.

Then a short 10th episode, still on the lines of Ep. 7 leads to the triple counterpoint in the position

$$\left\{ \begin{array}{l} \mathbf{A}\ \underset{1}{\wedge} \\ \mathbf{T}\ \underset{3}{\wedge} \\ \mathbf{B}\ \underset{2}{\wedge} \end{array} \right.$$

immediately followed by

$$\left\{ \begin{array}{l} \mathbf{S}\ \underset{1}{\wedge} \\ \mathbf{T}\ \underset{2}{\wedge} \\ \mathbf{B}\ \underset{3}{\wedge} \end{array} \right.$$

with which the fugue ends. It is a majestic and gorgeous movement which improves on acquaintance. But Bach evidently places no reliance on its triple counterpoint. And he seems to be impelled to think seriously and methodically about the rules by which a harmonic scheme can be totally inverted, having here proved by experience that you cannot safely invert a combination not made for the purpose. It is even possible that he had at first thought that this fugue would complete his scheme; and that all that follows is the result of his disappointment.

The next two fugues are *tours de force*, being compositions No. that can be inverted note for note from beginning to end. For XII purposes of comparison Bach writes his *Inversus* under his *Rectus*, so that you can see their relation as in a mirror. The difficulty of such counterpoint can be overrated. Suspensions, as Contrapunctus XI shows, must either be avoided or (as Bach was probably going to prove in the unfinished fugue, and as I prove in my conjectural finish) so contrived as to resolve both ways. A 4th from the treble will become a 4th from the bass and must be treated accordingly. Contrapunctus XIII is turned inside out as well as inverted, so that Treble=Bass, Alto—Treble, and Bass=Alto. This complicates the results of 5ths and 4ths so much that they must be treated as in triple counterpoint. Otherwise there are no special difficulties, and the composer only needs to watch the results of inversion without trusting only to rules of thumb, and he will achieve quite respectable music in both versions, though there may be no very clear evidence why either has been written at all.

Contrapunctus XII is a smooth little fugue of the simplest kind. The subject of K. d. F. is put into 3/2 time and, in the *Rectus*, is exposed in the order **B, T, A, S**, with a counter-subject that does not survive the exposition. Only 3 bars intervene between the soprano entry and the systematic exposition of a new variation of the theme.

Here are the two versions on one stave for purposes of
comparison:

Ex. 18.

S announces this variation in bar 21. It is answered by **A** in
G minor in bar 26. After a 2-bar interlude **T** has it in B♭
(bar 32). From bar 21 onwards it has been given a stretto-like
effect by close imitations in the other parts; but the fugue has
no really elaborate devices. Its only developed episode fills the
6 bars from 36 to 41, after which **B** enters with the varied theme
in D minor. A 4-bar episode separates this from the final
entry in the alto at bar 50.

The *Inversus* of course needs no separate analysis. It must
put its answer into the subdominant, for A minor becomes
G minor. Freedom in dealing with accidentals is essential: a
totally invertible harmony that renders semitone for semitone
is (*pace* Cherubini) a very poor pedantry. Bach's scheme is as
follows, with liberty as to accidentals:

Ex. 19.

Rectus.

Inver-
sion.

Though accidentals are handled freely, it is not permitted to
represent a diatonic semitone by a chromatic one: i.e. if two
notes are in alphabetical order in the *Rectus* (as G♭, F), they
must be in alphabetical order in the *Inversus* (as F, G♭).
On the other hand, Bach allows two F's an 8ve apart or
separated by a short rest, to be represented by an F♮ and an
F♯ in the inversion.

The whole scheme has some curious properties; for example,

in Ex. 20 the total inversion of (a) remains unchanged, while
(b) inverts into (c).

Ex. 20.

And Bach must have enjoyed a good laugh at the end of No. 12.
Rust (*Bach Ges. Jahr.* xxv) believes that Bach intended 'the
fugue which he had inverted note for note in all four parts' to
be the crown of the work. This is certainly not so; it is, for all
its astonishing 'slickness' (there is no other word for it), a very
simple affair, the simplest since Nos. I and II.

Contrapunctus XIII is in a much higher order of technique No.
and is a delightful piece of playful music. The last bar is the XIII.
only one in which *Inversus* is obviously not an original conception; and in the rest of the fugue the *Inversus* can have few
turns that could not occur in the *Rectus*, for the fugue is in
itself a fugue by inversion, like No. V, but without stretti. Its
subject is a brilliant comic variation of the filled-out K. d. F.
theme, as the following paradigm shows:

Ex. 21.

In the *Rectus* **A** opens with ∨. At the end of the fourth bar **B** answers with ∧; and 4 bars later **S** (which runs so high that Bach writes it in the treble clef instead of in the soprano used elsewhere in K. d. F.) completes the exposition with ∨. Episode 1 arises, like all the others, out of the fourth bar of ∨ and ∧. It fills 7 bars. The ∧ appears in **A**, followed by a 5-bar episode, in the last 2 bars of which **S** has 2 bars of ∧ in a subdominant aspect of B♭. (In the *Inversus* this becomes a dominant of F.) But the real entry is in **B** (end of bar 28) with ∨ in B♭. This is answered by **S** with ∧ in the same key, and followed by **A** with ∨ in G minor. The next episode leads in 7 bars, with some emphasis, back to D minor. The *Inversus* cannot achieve the same emphasis, though the running diminished 7th in bar 46 cleverly provides a dominant chord for both versions. At the end of bar 47 **A** (of *Rectus*) has ∧. Another episode leads in 8 bars to a rhetorical pause on the diminished 7th, the only form of dominant which remains dominant when inverted. Two more bars lead to ∨ in **B**, answered by the final entry of ∧ in **S**.

This analysis will of course apply to the *Inversus* by changing the signs and substituting **B** for **S**, **A** for **B**, and **S** for **A**.

Version for Two Claviers.

Bach was so pleased with both *Rectus* and *Inversus* of this fugue that he determined to make them playable. Totally invertible fugues cannot submit to the further restriction of being playable by two hands. Even if the stretches could be so confined, the parts have to cross in ways that could never be made clear on one keyboard. Bach did not arrange Contrapunctus XII; and its long-sustained notes do not suit keyboard music. It could be played, like my mirror-fugue in Appendix C, by an inverted string-quartet of one violin, viola, and two violoncellos.

But Contrapunctus XIII is simply asking to be played on two keyboard-instruments. Now, the two players have four

hands, and this fugue has only three parts. So Bach provides
a fourth part throughout, in both *Rectus* and *Inversus*; and even
fills up the rests in the exposition and elsewhere, thereby
showing how little he knows or cares about the orthodox
theory that the addition of an accompaniment to a fugue-
exposition annuls the fugue.

These free parts are the most astonishing *tour de force* in the
whole of K. d. F. Every rigid contrapuntal device that is not
merely crazy is child's-play to the task of providing a fourth
part to such counterpoint as this lively twin-pair of fugues. Of
course the free parts do not join in the scheme of total inversion. Their object is to make both fugues practically enjoyable
as pure works of art regardless of their structure. The resulting
clavier-versions, then, are not additions to the scheme of
K. d. F. but a means of removing both versions of Contrapunctus XIII into the world of independent music. The new
Bach-Gesellschaft edition makes three almost incredible blun-
ders here. First, it numbers the pair as another Contrapunctus.
It then prints them as mirror-fugues, with the free parts in the
same type as the rest—which obliterates the mirror-effect. It
finally crushes all four crossing parts into a reduction on two
staves which is as unplayable as two simultaneous Liszt con-
certos on one keyboard and as illegible as two snapshots on one
plate.

In the present edition it will be found that the small staves
and small print of the free parts do not interfere with the
mirror-effect of the score. And I myself had no idea of the
artfulness of these parts until I so disentangled them. In
the *Rectus* a free part actually seems to be able to share in the
fugue-subject, because it changes place with an essential part.

The clavier-versions themselves have always been inade-
quately edited in a point which here and in our pianoforte
edition is put right. We all know how dangerous it is to defer
crossing t's and dotting i's until one's task is otherwise finished.
The crossings and dottings of dotted quavers and semiquavers

are far more troublesome; and Handel never could be bothered with them. Yet we are constantly afflicted by learned editors who in preparing Handel for modern performance keep meticulously to every distinction between

$$\text{♪♪♪♩} \quad | \text{♪♪♩} \quad | \text{♪♪♩} |$$

when it is perfectly obvious that Handel never meant anything but ♪. ♪♪♩ every time. But that is an irritating hindrance to fluent penmanship, and even Bach has not always the patience to finish the last strokes and dots of such rhythms. I see, for instance, no reason to suppose that in the *Grave* of the C minor Clavier Partita the rhythm ♪♪♪♩ is ever intended, and I am sure that Bach always played and taught ♪. ♪♪♩ throughout.

Now we know that Contrapunctus XIII was written before the clavier versions. Bach could no more have written them first and then extracted the pure invertible fugues from them than David could have first written Psalm cxix in English and then extracted from it an alphabetical acrostic in Hebrew. That great Bach-scholar Rust himself loses his way in comparing the two versions. In another way his usual acumen deserts him. He meticulously preserves Bach's oversight in bar 46, where one group in the *Rectus* has lost its dots and crosses. Finding that the alto of *Inversus* slightly disagrees in this particular, Rust levels the parts up in the wrong direction. There is no reason in music why the prevailing rhythm should cease here, and plenty of reason in penmanship why it should cease here and anywhere when the writer is tired. Copy this pair of fugues in a hurry, especially in 2/4 time with twice as many group-bars, and see how often you wish the dots and crosses elsewhere!

The autograph of the clavier version is very close, very

rapid, and very firm, with no signs of the imminent breakdown of Bach's eyesight. He has evidently just begun to put in some dots and crosses. To suppose that he did not intend to complete the process as in Contrapunctus XIII is to follow the example of the monk who persisted in reading the non-existent word *mumpsimus* though everybody told him that it was a mistake for *sumpsimus*.

The editor's obvious duty is to carry out Bach's manifest intention here; and it would be easy to satisfy all consciences by citing the 57 places (I think I have counted right) where Bach has begun to put in the dots. But if any of my readers is a Mumpsimite I will not deprive him of the pleasure of independent research in this matter.

The Canons.

After Contrapunctus XIII the old editions (including Rust's B.-G. volume) give the earlier version of No. X and call it Contrapunctus XIV. Disregarding this, we come to the Canons. I confess that I am not clear as to Bach's purpose in writing such long movements in strict canon. Technically the problem is neither new nor useful. It is no more difficult to carry on a 2-part canon for 100 bars than to confine it to the length of a fugue-subject. The canons in *Das Musikalische Opfer* are much more difficult and also more like spontaneous works of art, because they are, with three exceptions, counterpoints to the *Canto fermo* of Frederick's theme. Of the exceptions the only long movement is the canonic fugue, written (though Bach, writing in enigmatic notation, does not say so) for flute, violin, and continuo. But there is no parallel elsewhere in Bach for the easygoing canons of *Die Kunst der Fuge*.

The Berlin autograph contains two, the inverse canon by augmentation and the canon in the 8ve. The latter it places before the triple-counterpoint fugue No. VIII, and this suggests that the canon in the 12th should precede the fugue in the 12th (No. IX) and the canon in the 10th should precede the fugue in the 10th (No. X). But Bach actually corrected the proofs of Nos. I to XI and let them be printed in their present order. We do not know whether he intended to write more canons than these four; and we do not know what he intended to demonstrate by them. Evidently those in the 12th and 10th illustrate the corresponding double counterpoints, because they are turned round so as to become canons in the 8ve. The inverse canon by augmentation might appropriately precede Contrapunctus VII. I confess to preferring its early version in Appendix B. The inverse augmentation there is reasonably melodious. In the final version we can only admire the beautiful counterpoint Bach builds on it as on an uncouth *canto fermo*. He is unhampered by any technical difficulty, for the follower lags more and more behind the leader, which can proceed as it likes, knowing that the consequences will not concern it, unless the composer attempts something not attempted here, the difficult task of making the canon really perpetual by getting the leader to run round twice while the augmentation goes once. This means that the leader must combine with both of the magnified halves of itself. In *Das Musikalische Opfer* Bach achieves this over the *canto fermo* of Frederick's theme, but only with extreme difficulty and with one actual (but remediable) oversight. Even the present easier problem is not artistic: no human ear or memory can trace an aesthetic relation between the absurd bass of bars 45–6 and the treble of bar 21. And all hope of defending the composition as beautiful counterpoint to a grotesque bass is dashed by Bach's plan of inverting the whole canon in double counter- point.

And so the Daddy-Longlegs sprawls in the treble until musical sense reappears in the 4-bar coda. The other canons are as good as such long unaccompanied canons can be, though they do not rival the equally long and exquisitely poetical F♯ minor slow movement of the A major sonata for cembalo and violin. They are smoother than the canons in the Goldberg

Variations; but those canons, like the canonic minuet and trio
in Mozart's C minor string quintet, or wind-octet, are the
more enjoyable for being cut up into square sections. Strict
canon lends itself to the purposes of epigram as naturally as
fugue lends itself to the purposes of architectural climax.

The most effective composition in the present four canons is
the lively 9/16 canon in the 8ve. All four canons begin with
gorgeous variations of the K. d. F. theme; and the 8ve canon
uses it in the direct as well as the inverted form. It makes an
amusing clavier-piece. The other canons would sound more
convincing on pairs of instruments with good vocal tone. That
in the 12th has the finest of all variations of our motto-theme,
except that in the unfortunate inverse augmented canon, of
which the opening might have served for a great slow movement.

The canon in the 10th begins with a fine illustration of the
cumulative effect of a long-limbed sequence rising in 3rds.
Why did Bach not show, when he inverted the whole in the
10th from bar 44 onwards, how either or both leader or follower
could be doubled in 3rds? The result would have been very
fine; but Bach has omitted to plan the small adjustments that
would be necessary, so we cannot suppose that he contemplated
it. However, his interest in this piece as a musical composition
leads him to provide it with a pause for an extempore cadenza;
and the obvious duty of the cadenza will be to illustrate this
possibility. In the pianoforte edition of the canons the editor
has supplied a dutiful cadenza accordingly.

I have put the canon in the 10th after instead of before that
in the 12th, so as to follow Bach's precedence of counterpoints.
And I have confined the title *Contrapunctus* to the fugues.
Bach, no doubt, would have called the canons 'tied-fugues'
(*fugae ligatae*) as distinguished from *recherché* fugues (*ricercare*).
So perhaps I am wrong in this detail. But further conjectures
about these canons are useless; one guess is as good as another,
and the topic is not important. We do not know whether

canons in more than two parts were contemplated, or whether the Art of Canon was not going to take as much space as the rest of the Art of Fugue. Perhaps Bach may have expected that in the higher orders of canon he would repeat his experience of the higher orders of fugue, and that the more intricate problems would solve themselves in the more expressive music. This is certainly the case outside K. d. F. Very little extra restriction would be needed to bring the whole *Qui tollis* of the B minor Mass into exact canonic form as a four-part vocal canon accompanied by a two-part instrumental one. Evidently between the extant K. d. F. canons and such a movement there is as great a distance as there is between Contrapunctus I and the unfinished quadruple Fugue.

Do the present four Canons show any feature of style which in the first place depends on their canonic form and in the second place contains the possibility of developing into things like the *Qui tollis* of the B minor Mass?

I think there is such a feature, and that it may be found in Mozart's C minor quintet, in the 'Hexen Menuet' of Haydn's D minor quartet Op. 76, No. 2, and in all the most serious as well as the wittiest of canons. It consists in making a rhetorical point of the way in which the leader pulls the follower after it, while the follower, in its turn, seems to egg the leader on to discover new ground to run over. Once begun the canon cannot stop; and this is either a fatal defect or an interesting quality. The extant K. d. F. canons make almost a joke of it; and that is as far as a long unaccompanied canon can go.

No. We now come to the mystery of the unfinished work. Here
XIV. conjecture is not at a loose end; the data are extraordinarily definite.

Bach left, in such connexion with the manuscript of K. d. F. that his family and first editors had no doubt of its relevance, an enormous unfinished fugue. Before it breaks off it is already longer than any other of Bach's fugues. It contains three subjects, the last being based on the name BACH in German musical nomenclature where B is B♭ and H is B♮. Bach's last 7 bars contain the first combination of the three themes. The original edition breaks off 7 bars earlier; why, nobody can say; any more than why it ignores Bach's proof-corrections and alters his significant special title to his last organ-chorale.

Rust and others, noting the absence of the K. d. F. theme, argued that this fugue does not belong to the work, and that Bach had really finished it, regarding the simple little 4-part mirror-fugue as the crown of the whole. Nottebohm, the decipherer of Beethoven's sketch-books, settled that question by discovering that the K. d. F. theme combines with the other three in a manner quite beyond the possibility of chance, the quaver tail of the theme even filling out a halt in the rhythm of the rest of the combination. Riemann accordingly embodies Nottebohm's discovery in a short coda making no pretensions to artistic composition.

Now what does the earliest tradition say? Mizler, writing in 1754, only four years after Bach's death, says: 'His last illness prevented him from completing according to plan the last fugue but one, and from working out the last, which was to contain 4 themes and to be inverted note for note continuously [*nachgehends*] in all 4 parts' (*apud* B–G, XXV, p. xviii).

Rust says that this is impossible. Compositions like Contrapunctus XII can have no suspended discords and cannot be extended to the length of a quadruple fugue. Bach must have meant that that four-part fugue which he had already inverted note for note was to be the crown of the work. He must often have said so in his last illness; and of course his wife and daughters and the 15-year-old son Johann Christian, who constituted his household at the time, understood nothing about such learned music and could not fail to spread errors broadcast when they tried to talk about it.

I see no reason to suppose that Mrs. Bach and the boy Johann Christian did not understand Bach's intentions quite

as well as he expressed them. Mrs. Bach sang all her husband's
soprano music, and wrote a musical hand which is hard to tell
from his. Johann Christian was a better musician at 15 than
I was, and I should have had no difficulty at his age in under-
standing whether Bach meant what Mizler said or what Rust
thinks he meant. If I had been one of Bach's household at 15,
he would probably have been exercising me and Johann
Christian in score-playing with each fugue as soon as it was
written. And Mizler's statement has a very different kind of
precision from the picturesqueness of legends.

From this point the most interesting way to reach a conclusion is by analysing the fugue as far as Bach finished it, and
then describing how its data lead to a finish on the lines
followed by me, and how, in connexion with Mizler's statement, they indicate the project of another fugue on the lines of
my mirror-fugue in Appendix C.

The mighty composition which I call Contrapunctus XIV
begins with a section 115 bars long, on one of the severest
themes ever invented. We may call it the *canto fermo* theme.
The great C♯ minor fugue, with its 3 subjects and its enormous
stretto, is exactly the length of this one section.

The exposition is (as usual in K. d. F. and rather unusual
elsewhere) quite uninterrupted, and in the order **B, T, A, S**,
at the 6-bar intervals filled by the subject. Note the tonal
answer, with the repeated note which the dotted minim makes
possible as it was not possible with the crotchets of Contrapunctus XI. There is no counter-subject; but a prevalent
crotchet figure

is evidently derived from the first four notes of the subject, by
free diminution. Such derivations are valid according to their
immediate context. These same four notes may be found later

as parts of another theme with no reference to (a) in their intention. Immediately after the exposition there is a stretto of **B** $\lor$ and **T** $\land$ at 3 bars. One bar this **A** has $\lor$, followed after a bar's interlude by stretto 2. Here **B** precedes **S** with an allusion to the first 4 notes, but the real stretto is between **S** $\land$ (tonal answer) and **A** $\land$ (subject) at 1 bar. Immediately afterwards **B** has $\land$ in F (approached from C). After a 7-bar episode on figure (a) **T** $\lor$ enters in G minor followed by Stretto 3, which is the converse of Stretto 2, viz. **B** $\land$ (subject), answered tonally by **S** $\land$. A 2-bar interlude leads to Stretto 4, the inverse-contrary of Stretti 1 and 2, viz.: **A** $\lor$ answered tonally at 1 bar by **T** $\lor$, in B$\flat$. After a bar's interlude Stretto 5 appears in D minor: **S** $\land$ answered at 2 bars by **A** $\land$. An episode on a new line leads in $3\frac{1}{2}$ bars to Stretto 6. This is in 3 parts, beginning in B$\flat$ with **B** $\land$ answered at 1 bar by **T**, which, beginning with an inversion, changes its direction after the fourth note. At the third bar of the **B** subject, **A** $\land$ enters in G minor, crossing over the soprano —to the confusion of early editors. Their error is rectified in the new Bach-Ges. edition. Stretto 7 immediately follows in D minor. It is in 3 parts and very close, consisting of a new answer-position of **T** $\land$, answered at half a bar by **S** $\lor$ (with an ornament in bar 101) and at 2 bars by **A** $\land$. After a 2-bar interlude there is a solitary final entry of **B** $\land$, accompanied by (a) in dialogue above. Four more bars close this great first section. Through the last chord runs the beginning of $\underset{2}{\land}$ in **A**. This is a rich coloratura theme filling 7 bars. At the eighth bar **S** answers in the dominant, and **B** and **T** follow regularly. Six bars after this exposition we have the combination $\begin{cases} \mathbf{S}\ \underset{2}{\land} \\ \mathbf{B}\ \underset{1}{\land} \end{cases}$. It is answered after a 3-bar interlude by $\begin{cases} \mathbf{A}\ \underset{2}{\land} \\ \mathbf{T}\ \underset{1}{\land} \end{cases}$ in A minor. When $\underset{1}{\land}$ is combined with other themes it is singularly difficult to manage in any other part than the bass, and Bach has to double-dot its second note before he can find a proper bass for it. An episode of 5 bars arises from the last figure of $\underset{2}{\wedge}$.

Ex. 22.

Then we have what looks like the D–C inversion of the pair in the 8ve. It is in F major $\begin{cases} \mathbf{S} \underset{1}{\wedge} \\ \mathbf{T} \underset{2}{\wedge} \end{cases}$. But it is a new combination; for $\underset{1}{\wedge}$ enters a bar too late. A 6-bar episode leads to another new combination in G minor: $\mathbf{B} \underset{2}{\wedge}$ with $\mathbf{A} \underset{1}{\wedge}$ a bar late and in stretto with $\mathbf{S} \underset{1}{\wedge}$ (tonal answer moving to C minor) at 1 bar. Six more bars close this section in G minor, and introducing $\underset{b}{\vee}$ as well as $\underset{b}{\wedge}$.

The third subject now enters. It begins with Bach's own name B (♭), A, C, H (=B♮), to which it adds a turn which makes the theme a chromatic phrase in D minor. This is announced by **T,** and answered in stretto by **A.** Its continuation

(x)

is not meant to remind us of (a). **S** enters 6 bars after the beginning of **A** and is answered at 2 bars by **B.** After the fourth bar of **B** there is a 3-bar interlude on (x). The **T** enters. (I cannot agree with Busoni that the syncopated soprano of bars 211–13 is intended to allude to $\underset{V}{1}$, which would be quite irrelevant here unless it could be followed up.) **T** is answered at 3 bars by $\mathbf{A} \overset{3}{\underset{V}{}}$. This inversion is not according to the scale of Ex. 19, but on the following scheme:

Ex. 23.

&c.

Then we have a close stretto of $\wedge_3$ between **S** and **B** at the half-bar. The bass has to expand one note from a minim to a semibreve. It then gives $\underset{\vee}{3}$: closing into C, where another close stretto ($\wedge_3$ syncopated in **T** with **A** in normal rhythm after 3 crotchets) returns to D minor. Three crowded bars, with something like a diminution of x, end the section with a half-close.

The fourth section now begins with the 3 subjects in the combination

$$\begin{cases} \mathbf{A}\,\wedge_2 \\ \mathbf{T}\,\wedge_3 \\ \mathbf{B}\,\wedge_1 \end{cases}$$

S freely imitates $\wedge_2$. Bach's autograph breaks off with $\wedge_b$ in the tenor. What was his intention for the sequel? Three things are certain. First, the theme of K. d. F. was to make the combination a quadruple counterpoint. Secondly, neither $\wedge_1$ nor $\underset{\vee}{1}$ are in double counterpoint at the 8ve with the others. Bach himself found it difficult (as we have seen) even to get $\wedge_1$ into an inner part in combination with $\wedge_2$. In the deferred position of bars 169–74 it will combine with $\wedge_3$ as well as with $\wedge_2$, but will not then also combine with the fourth theme. Thirdly, the movement must not again be interrupted in order to give the fourth subject a separate exposition. That would be a fatal error of composition. The entry of $\wedge_2$ has brought back quaver-movement; we are certainly entering upon the final section of the work, and nothing must stop its flow. Moreover, to introduce the new theme as a surprise without interruption is the one device of composition still in reserve for this juncture. Contrapunctus IX introduced it early, without interrupting the fugue by so much as a half-close. Slightly less certain than these 3 points is the main assumption underlying my composition of the whole peroration. I am absolutely certain that Bach

intended to invert all 4 themes in the quadruple counterpoint;
and the only possible doubt is whether this was to happen in
the present fugue or in the other which Mizler says was
projected. In $\wedge_2$ the following notes

Ex. 24.

show every sign of being constructed for inverse-contrary
counterpoint. Melodically they are artificial, though construable
enough, and their evident purpose is to make accented discords
that resolve both ways, downwards within one crotchet in the
original position, downwards at the minim when inverted. And
I think that the total inversions were to happen in this fugue,
because it requires a peroration of at least 80 bars, and this
gives plenty of room for all the variety we can obtain from the
now incessant whirl of the quadruple counterpoint.

I begin by immediately answering Bach's three-part combination with an A minor entry of

$$\left\{ \begin{array}{l} \text{S } \wedge_3 \\ \text{A } \wedge_1 \text{ in 12th.} \\ \text{T } \wedge_2 \end{array} \right.$$

There must be millions of chances in favour of the assumption
that the treatment of $\wedge_1$ in the 12th represents Bach's intention.

One theme may work accidentally in the 12th with one other,
but hardly with two, and certainly not with three.

An episode (on $\vee_b$ and $\wedge_b$) leads in 5 bars to an inverse-
contrary combination in A minor:

$$\left\{ \begin{array}{l} \text{S } \vee_2 \\ \text{A } \vee_1 \text{ in 12th.} \\ \text{B } \vee_3 \end{array} \right.$$

(Not being Busoni, I cannot make up Bach's mind to force $\vee_3$
into exact semitonic correspondence by putting F♯ against the

F♮ in $\underset{\vee}{1}$. Bach is not afraid of such collisions, as the wonderful slow movement of the first Brandenburg concerto drastically shows; but he draws the line sharply at taking them by skip.)[1]

The fourth theme must not enter too soon, but we have now deferred it for 3 entries, and must prepare for it. Five bars on $\underset{\vee}{\flat}$ and $\underset{\flat}{\wedge}$ lead with emphatic steps back to D minor. The alto, made conspicuous by striking an 8ve with the soprano, now delivers the K. d. F. theme in the inverse-contrary 4-part combination

---

[1] The reader will expect some comment on Busoni's great *Fantasia Contrapuntistica*, which contains the whole extant portion of Bach's unfinished fugue, developed not to an end of its own but to the purposes of a much larger work. It seems unusual, even with acknowledgements, to absorb 238 bars (or more than 10 minutes) of pure Bach into a modern composition; and I cannot work up any enthusiasm for compositions or cadenzas that purport to review the progress of music since classical times. Modern styles aspire to a purity of their own: introduced into older styles they are mere impurities. Bach's own style would be a ghastly impurity if introduced into a Palestrina Mass. With contrapuntal forms there is really neither interest nor technical merit in merely taking advantage of modern possibilities as licences. A genuinely modern polyphony requires modern material.

Of course Busoni is able to combine the themes of this fugue casually with everything else in K. de F., to make brilliant inexact stretti on $\underset{2}{\wedge}$, and, as observed above, to preserve the chromatic character of $\underset{\vee}{3}$ even where this means taking B♮ by skip against B♭.

Our present task is not to produce a review of musical progress since Bach, but to follow the humbler and higher aim of carrying out what is discoverable of Bach's actual intentions.

Where my combinations are the same as Busoni's this is because in those features Busoni was also working out Bach's own design. I did not know the *Fantasia Contrapuntistica* when I worked out my conjectures. But if I had known Busoni's work I should have had no more scruple in coinciding with his true combinations than in copying the finished part of Bach's fugue. And of course I no more dispute his priority than I dispute Nottebohm's or Riemann's.

This is followed, after a bar's interlude, by the direct combination

$$
\left\{
\begin{array}{l}
\text{S } \underset{1}{\wedge} \text{ in 12th.} \\
\text{A} \underset{3}{\wedge} \\
\text{T} \underset{2}{\wedge} \\
\text{B} \underset{4}{\wedge}
\end{array}
\right.
$$

(It will be seen that $\underset{1}{\wedge}$ must be in the 12th when it is not in the bass, and $\overset{1}{\vee}$ must be in the 12th when it is not in the soprano.) A 3-bar interlude (still on $\underset{b}{\wedge}$ and $\overset{b}{\vee}$) leads to the inverted combination

$$
\left\{
\begin{array}{l}
\text{S } \overset{3}{\vee} \\
\text{A} \overset{2}{\vee} \\
\text{T} \overset{4}{\vee} \\
\text{B} \overset{1}{\vee} \text{ in 12th.}
\end{array}
\right.
$$

Another 3 bars (on another figure of $\underset{2}{\wedge}$) lead to A minor, with the direct position

$$
\left\{
\begin{array}{l}
\text{S } \underset{2}{\wedge} \\
\text{A} \underset{3}{\wedge} \\
\text{T} \underset{4}{\wedge} \\
\text{B} \underset{1}{\wedge}
\end{array}
\right.
$$

Now it is evident that both $\underset{1}{\wedge}$ and $\overset{1}{\vee}$ are, in spite of their capacity for inversion in the 12th, most at ease in the bass. Accordingly **B** tends to have more than its share of them. This fact had better be turned to rhetorical purpose; and so the climax is brought about by the following steps in which $\underset{1}{\wedge}$ moves up in the bass from a low dominant to a final tonic.

Ex. 25.

The quadruple combination having finished at bar 295, the upper parts continue first with $\wedge$ and $\vee_b$ in the soprano, and then with 3-part imitations of $\wedge_a$. At bar 305 the final combination appears:

$$
\begin{array}{l}
\mathbf{S}\ \wedge_4 \\
\mathbf{A}\ \wedge_2 \\
\mathbf{T}\ \wedge_3 \\
\mathbf{B}\ \wedge_1
\end{array}
$$

and on the final tonic pedal Bach's signature appears on the top with the latter portions of $\wedge_4$ and $\wedge_2$ in the middle parts.

Appendix.

Appendix A contains the chorale-prelude which Bach dictated on his death-bed. In harmonies of childlike simplicity and beauty, three lower parts treat each phrase of the chorale in fugue by inversion until the soprano gives the phrase in long notes above. The reader should make his own analysis. Only four letters are required, one for each phrase of the tune: capitals for the *canto fermo* in the soprano, and small letters for the other parts. The signs $\wedge$ and $\vee$ will be required throughout, together with the sign $\square$ when figure (d) is given in crotchets as well as in quavers.

The bars in which the *canto fermo* is present are transcribed, without the original florid ornamentation, from a setting without interludes in the *Orgelbüchlein*. Bach dictated the new interludes on his death-bed in a room darkened to spare his suffering eyes.

The original editors of K. d. F. gave this wonderful piece as a compensation for leaving the last fugue unfinished. Rust's description of the manuscript in B.G. XXV. ii is a beautiful little biographical essay.

Appendix B is the earlier version of the canon by inverse augmentation.

Conjectural Finale.

Appendix C is the final step in the vindication of Mizler. He may have made a mistake and, hearing that the unfinished fugue was to be on 4 invertible subjects, may have confused this with an invertible fugue on 4 subjects. That was my first idea of what happened; but I can see no reason why Mizler should not have been right. One does not from mere confusion draw Mizler's explicit distinction between an unfinished last fugue but one and an unwritten last fugue. Rust's *a priori* objection is not evidence. *Solvitur ambulando.*

If this fugue existed, what would its themes be? Two of them we know; one must have been the K. d. F. theme and another must have been B, A, C, H. I am sure that the fugue was not going to be written on the four themes of the unfinished fugue. Even if Bach had not intended already to use the inverse-contrary positions in that fugue, there would be no point in working out the same themes in a pair of mirror-fugues. Moreover, I cannot find two positions of that quadruple counterpoint that will go into exact mirror-relationship to each other; though I confess that I have not the patience for an exhaustive search. But tonal accommodations, free play of joints, and inversions in the 12th are of no avail to produce mirror-fugues. Nor, on the other hand, do I believe that Bach found his combinations by exhaustive mechanical search. I think that when he composed the unfinished fugue he began by making a draft of exactly my bars 306–10 (except for the free final joints), and thought how fine it would be if his bass was not under the usual necessity of avoiding complete chords with the upper parts but could invert in the 12th and so have a firm 5th above it whenever the harmony would be the better for it. I am also certain that he found himself obliged (unlike Riemann) to syncopate the third bar of the K. d. F. theme; and I should be astonished if he found that beyond this isolated detail any other variation was workable. The detail looks anomalous on paper, but does not worry the ear at all; and, in spite of his uncanny schematic exactness, nobody wrote more truly for the ear and more independently of the eye than Bach.

Mizler's supposed last fugue, then, must have been on a new combination. I have tried experiments with other themes whose capacity has not been exhausted in K. d. F.

Contrapunctus X, for example, gives only one side of a matter that has at least four; and, apart from that, it is hard to believe that such an approximation as this could happen by accident.

Ex. 26.

which inverts into this:

Ex. 27

But here Bach's name must always clip its first note into a

crotchet, because the beautiful suspension of the dotted minim
against it will not invert. Yet the suspension is necessary to
explain the doubled 4th at *. And the theme of Contrapunctus
X is compelled to drift into something very like the latter part of
$\bigwedge_{2}$ in the unfinished fugue. This will never do. Nothing is
more astonishing in K. d. F. than the complete absence of
unmotived recurrence of phrase or mannerism in 14 fugues
and 4 canons all on the same subject, in the same key, and in
pure part-writing.

I do not claim to have exhausted the possibilities; but I think
the attempt unnecessary when the probability is that any final
fugue Bach had in mind was at least as different from the others
as they are from each other. Unless we regard a mirror-fugue
as two fugues, the only fugues that are related as pairs are the
couples VI–VII and VIII–XI. This gives no ground for
thinking that the last fugue was to pair with any others. And
so I have proceeded on new lines.

First, a few more words must be devoted to the question of
total inversion. As has already been said, its difficulty has been
grossly overrated. And that difficulty is much lessened and
the resources greatly increased if the style is chromatic. The
extant mirror-fugues are diatonic. This creates a strong presumption that the final fugue was to be chromatic. Nearly any
chromatic harmony that proceeds (like Bach's) by semitones,
will invert into something tolerable. For instance, here is the
Tugendqual Motif from Wagner's unwritten *Tantris und Solide*,
though some believe it to be the *Abgeschiedene-Vielfrassweis'*
mentioned in *Die Meistersinger* (Ex. 28).

This becomes more familiar when inverted (Ex. 29). I am
sorry for the Spohr-like inner part of the last bar; but pure
Wagner will not invert, any more than a random extract of
Bach himself.

It is no use speculating as to what can be done with total
inversion in post-Wagnerian harmony: where there are no
rules there are no difficulties; and where there are arbitrary

Ex. 28.

Langweilig und schamlos.

Ex. 29.

Langsam und schmachtend.

systems you can get just as good another arbitrary system by turning your music upside down. Anything that sounds no better right-side up than upside down will do for an up-to-date piece of totally invertible counterpoint.

Bach wrote many things that Wagner would have thought
bold; such as the following episode from an unfinished fugue
in C minor:

Ex. 30.

But this is not Wagnerian; and Wagner's wonderful suggestions of remote tonality by means of long appoggiaturas would,
I believe, have seemed to Bach like a new kind of false relation.
Some such effects often turned up in my first sketches for
Appendix C; and a sufficiency of them might have made a
consistent style on Wagnerian lines. But, though I was at no
pains here to keep to Bach's language I could not think fit to
take the task so easily, and I have therefore eliminated everything that I could suppose would annoy Bach. For a short
chromatic fugue on so rich a plan as is implied by the use of
4 subjects the most natural style would be emotionally highly
charged; and so one of my original themes is declamatory.

Ex. 31.

In order to present the *Inversus* with better opportunities for
a convincing top-part, I base my normal quadruple counterpoint on the inversion of this theme, so that it comes right-side
up in the *Inversus*, in places where the *Rectus* has the other
three themes direct.

My other original theme is in the style of Bach's 3-part
Invention (Sinfonia) in F minor:

Ex. 32.

Then, of course, there is the theme of K. d. F., which I give in the following rhythm:

and Bach's name:

There is no room for episodes; nor can we afford four separate expositions. With every permissible means of compression this fugue, if it is to be a composition in any proper sense of the word, will take nearly 100 slow bars. (It actually takes 96.)

The analysis of the *Rectus* is as follows:

The exposition of $\wedge_1$ takes the order **T, B**, a bar's interlude, **S, A** (with a subdominant answer). After a 2-bar interlude **B** enters with $\vee_1$ and **T** gives out the B, A, C, H, theme $\wedge_2$. On the last note begins the reverse combination, **T** $\wedge$ with **A** $\vee^2$. After this **S** enters with $\wedge_2$, and the first subject is abandoned. Then **B** completes this second exposition by entering with $\vee^2$. After a 3-bar interlude there is a close stretto, at intervals of 2 beats, with **A** $\wedge_2$, **S** $\vee^2$, and **B** $\vee^2$. Three more bars bring the first main section of the fugue to a close in the tonic. Through its last chord **A** announces a diminished version of the K. d. F. theme, answered in stretto, and by inversion, by **T** and **S**. After 4 bars of this the full-sized theme $\wedge_3$ enters in **B** accompanied by $\vee_3$ and $\wedge_3$. On its last note **T** answers it, and **S** announces $\wedge_4$. Again the last note overlaps with the combination $\left\{ \begin{array}{l} \textbf{S } \wedge_3 \\ \underline{\textbf{A}} \wedge_4 \end{array} \right.$, and this overlaps by yet another bar the combinition $\begin{cases} \text{A} \stackrel{\wedge}{3} \\ \text{T} \stackrel{\wedge}{4} \end{cases}$. A close stretto (at one minim) on $\stackrel{\wedge}{4}$ then occupies all 4 parts for 5 bars, ending emphatically on the dominant. Then a second skirmish of stretto in diminution, this time with $\stackrel{\wedge}{8}$ and $\stackrel{\vee}{7}$ as well as $\stackrel{\wedge}{8}$ and $\stackrel{\vee}{7}$, leads in 5 bars to the quadruple counterpoint. The first position is

$$\begin{cases} \text{S} \stackrel{\wedge}{\substack{1\\2}} \\ \text{A} \stackrel{\vee}{} \\ \text{T} \stackrel{\vee}{4} \\ \text{B} \stackrel{\vee}{3} \end{cases}$$

It is immediately answered by

$$\begin{cases} \text{S} \stackrel{\wedge}{3} \\ \text{A} \stackrel{\wedge}{2} \\ \text{T} \stackrel{\wedge}{\substack{4\\1}} \\ \text{B} \stackrel{\vee}{} \end{cases}$$

A 2-bar interlude is followed by

$$\begin{cases} \text{S} \stackrel{\vee}{4} \\ \text{A} \stackrel{\wedge}{1} \\ \text{T} \stackrel{\wedge}{3} \\ \text{B} \stackrel{\wedge}{2} \end{cases}$$

to which **S** adds, by way of filling up the first bar, $\stackrel{\wedge}{8}$. (This diminution was the way out of a trivial difficulty. Often the one really unobtrusive way round an awkward harmonic corner is by a canonic device.)

Four more bars end in a climax on Bach's useful and imperturbably invertible diminished 7th. Then, after a pause, 4 bars in broken rhythm lead to the final combination

$$\begin{cases} \text{S} \stackrel{\wedge}{4} \\ \text{A} \stackrel{\wedge}{2} \\ \text{T} \stackrel{\wedge}{\substack{3\\1}} \\ \text{B} \stackrel{\vee}{} \end{cases}$$

after which the imitative 3-bar *adagio* close alludes to the inverted K. d. F. theme.

The complete scheme of K. d. F. would appear to be as follows:

I. Four simple fugues, two upon $\wedge$ and two upon $\vee$; the latter pair comprising (*a*) a chromatic fugue with a counter-subject and a variation; and (*b*) a study in highly developed episodes.

II. Three stretto-fugues, one by inversion, one by diminution and inversion, and one by augmentation, diminution, and inversion.

III. Three fugues in the principal orders of double counter-point, (*a*) a triple fugue in the 8ve; (*b*) a double fugue in the 12th; (*c*) a double fugue in the 10th (and, incidentally, in the 12th).

IV. Studies in total inversion, (*a*) a fugue freely inverting the triple counterpoint of the former triple fugue; (*b*) a strictly invertible simple fugue in 4 parts, with a variation of the subject; (*c*) a strictly invertible 3-part fugue by contrary motion, with the parts reversible in an inside-out order; and with subsequently added free parts outside the invertible scheme.

V. Two quadruple fugues, one with 4 invertible subjects of which 1 is in the 12th; and the other a totally invertible fugue with 4 subjects. (My effort at this also contains diminutions and stretti.)

VI. Four canons which Bach seems to have thought of attaching to the four fugues in the corresponding orders of counterpoint. He abandoned this intention if he ever had it, and we do not know whether these are all the canons in his plan, or what their function is.

Does K. d. F. contain every kind of fugue that interests Bach? It is noticeable that he almost never *professedly* writes the kind of double fugue that begins with two themes at once. The only mature examples I know are that at the end of the Passacaglia and the second movement of the C major Sonata for two violins; and I can recall only one other example, very early and not important. On the other hand, he would have been quite justified in calling the main part of the E♭ Prelude, W. K., I. 7 (from bar 25 onwards) a double fugue, and the A major Prelude, W. K., I. 17, and the three-part F minor Invention triple fugues of this kind.

Bach's choruses often contain a type of fugue hardly possible within the limits of four keyboard parts. We may call it a round-fugue. In a chorus with free orchestral accompaniment, or a double-chorus motet, let one voice start a coloratura fugue-subject. Let it accompany the next voice with a counter-subject, and a second counter-subject, and a third, and so on till the exposition is complete. Then let the chorus continue to treat the result like a round that oscillates between tonic and dominant. Two more entries will have made a big continuous section; and, if this has reached the dominant or any other key, the orchestra may intervene with a ritornello, and the round may be resumed once more and finished in the tonic. The form thus mapped out can exist with quite as solid an effect if the later counter-subjects are obliterated.

Such is the structure of the huge first Kyrie of the B minor Mass, and (after the massive introductory sequences) of the *Et in terra pax* and *Cum sancto spiritu*. The great isolated double chorus *Nun ist das Heil* is on this plan and preserves a sextuple counterpoint.

Figured chorale-fugues are also outside the scope of *Die Kunst der Fuge* as their subjects change but do not combine.

With these exceptions *Die Kunst der Fuge* is a complete demonstration of what Bach understood by the term Fugue as applied to whole compositions and not merely as a kind of texture used here and there. It cannot be too strongly insisted that *Die Kunst der Fuge* is, for by far the most part, normal keyboard music dealing with the central elements of Bach's art, in his latest and most perfect style, and with his fullest power of free composition on a large scale.

PART II

THE above analysis has dealt with K. d. F. from a single point of view from which no wide digressions have been made. But there are other points of view less central and therefore less amenable to connected argument, but none the less insistent in their claims to attention. Some of them are discussed here.

I. *The Berlin Autograph in relation to the order of the Fugues and Canons.*

In Bach-Ges. XXV. 1 will be found a list (reproduced in the new B.-G.) of the readings peculiar to the Berlin autograph. Without exception they are details which Bach deliberately altered afterwards; and in some cases the alterations are made on the autograph itself. One point makes orthographic history, viz. the systematic correction, in Contrapunctus 7, of the old inaccurate notation ♩.♫ (which so many modern editors take for a triplet) into the accurate ♪♫, a point explicitly referred to in the final docket 'Corrigirt'. The *stile Francese* was becoming old-fashioned, but Leopold Mozart had not yet persuaded musicians to adopt the double dot.

The autograph is not in open score and suggests no doubt that the music was for the keyboard. The order of the pieces proves nothing except that the only admissible order is that of the printed edition as far as Contrapunctus XI. Probably the pieces stand in the autograph in the order in which they were composed. If this is so, it would seem that Bach started with the intention that Contrapunctus I, on the direct subject, should be followed by the fugue on the inverted subject (now Contrapunctus III); but that the idea of the present Contrapunctus II interrupted his further plans. For Contrapunctus II, which stands third in the 'Berlin autograph', is manifestly less highly organized than Contrapunctus III. Be this as it may, Bach at first put Contrapunctus II in the third place and ended it with a half-close at bar 78. So it must have been meant to lead to something else; preferably not Contrapunctus V, which here stands next to it, and which, with all its stretti, is a smooth and quiet affair in a milder dotted rhythm which is neither a match nor a contrast to that of Contrapunctus II. The present Contrapunctus IV, according to my view of it as a lively *alla breve*, would follow the truncated or completed Contrapunctus II well enough; but there is no trace of this fourth fugue in the Berlin autograph. It is significant, however, that the present IV and V both begin on the dominant as required by the truncated dominant close of II.

After the present Contrapunctus V came the fugue in the 12th (Contrapunctus IX), noted in common time with quavers and semiquavers, but already docketed with an instruction to change to *alla breve*.

Then followed the fugue in the 10th (Contrapunctus X), written in common-time bars and notes of half the printed values, and beginning with the soprano alone at bar 23.

After these examples of higher contrapuntal orders came the two fugues by diminution and augmentation (Contrapunctus VI and VII); followed by the $\frac{9}{16}$ canon in the 8ve, first written as a riddle, giving only the leading part and a sign for the entry of the answer, and then written again in full.

The triple fugue (Contrapunctus VIII) and the fugue on the same three subjects inexactly inverted (Contrapunctus XI) now followed in a juxtaposition which is the only point in which the Berlin autograph has a logical advantage over the score. The notation is $\frac{2}{4}$ with notes of half the printed value; and a pencil instruction at the head of Contrapunctus VIII provides for the change.

The augmented canon, as in Appendix B, came next; written twice, first as in Appendix B, secondly as a puzzle canon with only the leading part written out and no provision for the inversion in double-counterpoint. In this form the puzzle is misleading, especially in its title of 'per augmentationem perpetuus', for this should imply that the bass produces the whole leader by inverted augmentation instead of only its first half. And the bass can do no such thing, as experiment will show.

Then come the mirror fugues, likewise in $\frac{3}{4}$ and $\frac{2}{4}$ respectively. There is no instruction to change the notation, but I am philistine enough to see no reason why the original edition should not take the instruction for granted, as it did. But it should not have printed the mirror-fugues in succession instead of in mirror-reflection, nor should it have put the Inversus of XII before the Rectus. Commentators, however, go too far when they argue that the Rectus and Inversus of XIII are also in the wrong order, on the assumption that the Rectus should begin with the direct subject. It is a matter of complete indifference which version of the subject is taken either for a whole fugue or as the beginning of a fugue in contrary motion. Fugues II and IV are not inverse fugues though their subject is the inversion of that of I and III. The subject of each fugue is its own business, regardless of what it may be in another fugue. The question which of the mirror-fugues is Rectus and which Inversus can be settled by a glance at the close of each. The difference between an original idea and an artificial derivation is unmistakable.

The Berlin autograph ends with the augmented canon in its final form, but still in common time with bars of double the printed length and half the note-values.

Attached to the Berlin autograph are three supplements:

1. The final version of the augmented canon on paper prepared for use in engraving, though not for the actual plates of the first edition. C. P. E. Bach attests that his father altered the title on a proof-plate from *Canon per Augment. in Contrapuncto all Octava* into *Canon p. Augmentationem contrario motu.*

2. The Clavier fugues derived from the second pair of mirror-fugues. The free parts are inserted *currenti calamo*, and squeezed in between the rest.

3. The unfinished fugue, written (like the rest of these supplements) on one side of the paper. On the back of the fourth of its five leaves is Bach's autograph list of misprints which corrects the original edition from the beginning of Contrapunctus VIII to the middle of Contrapunctus XI, and thereby removes all shadow of doubt as to Bach's final intentions up to that point. After that point the original edition violently divests itself of all authority by its treatment of the mirror-fugues. Bach can never have meant to publish the early version of Contrapunctus X. So nothing remains for us but to put the great unfinished fugue last and to arrange the four canons before it. I have given a reason for the trivial detail that the canon in the 10th should follow that in the 12th; for the rest I can only confess that the more I see of the canon in the 10th and the final version of the augmented canon the less I understand them. In the canon in the 10th I can find neither aesthetic nor technical cogency in bars 22–39, which are harmonically thin and unrhetorical, and which wreck the otherwise promising possibility of developing euphonious harmony by doubling either part in 3rds, 6ths, or 10ths; and after editing Appendix B for the pianoforte I am amazed at the indisputable fact that Bach rejected it in favour of the canon eventually printed. All this makes it the more probable that these canons were only the beginning of a development of which we know nothing. Those in the 12th and 10th are not in the Berlin autograph, which otherwise contains the whole work except Contrapunctus IV.

A complete set of canons would have made an admirable set of preludes to these figures. In the mid-nineteenth century Klengel executed a similar idea in his 48 Canons and Fugues. His canons sometimes turned out better than his fugues; because the canons, like Bach's, refused to sit down; whereas

you can Klengelize any Bach fugue by squaring up its phrases
and putting a full close at every phrase thus squared. And so
we come to two other topics: the uses and misuses of counterpoint, and how to find preludes for these fugues.

II. *Contrapuntal Devices, useful and useless.*

I confess that I enjoyed writing my quadruple mirror-fugue.
But nothing less than the hope of thinking Bach's thoughts
after him would have induced me to enter on such a task; and
I do not recommend it as an exercise. We need not hope to
capture Bach's spirit by wrestling with his technique. But, as
Bach's uncle pointed out in eight-part choral music with
Scripture warrant for his text, it is good for Jacob to wrestle
with an angel; and we shall certainly not earn Bach's blessing
by declining to learn what can be known of his technique.

Now there is no doubt that Bach thought mirror-counterpoint a useful exercise, at all events for himself, if not for less
advanced students. Did he, then, set no limits to the abstruse-
ness of his problems? Did he never ask whether there was a
point beyond which technique degenerates into idle mechanism?

Nobody will be so insensitive as to deny the beauty of most
of Bach's inverted themes and inverted two-part combinations.
Purcell, Bach, and Brahms have in common this feature of style
that they often conceive melodies that invert into melodies
equally (and sometimes differently) expressive. When the
main forms of music are those of diatonic counterpoint, such
melodies are as likely to occur to the composer as any others, for
his technique is largely a habitual accuracy in measuring the
ups and downs by which desirable harmonic notes can be
reached by good melodic rhetoric, and vice versa. It is less
difficult to understand why melodic inversion is so common in
Purcell, Bach, and Brahms, than to account for its being only
an occasional device in Palestrina, Handel, and Mozart. Perhaps we are here encountering a result of the fact that Palestrina

and Handel are masters who regard an art-form as a scaffolding, a means by which works of art can be erected but which neither creates them nor survives them; whereas to Bach and Brahms the form and the matter are inseparable aspects of the whole. But this leaves Purcell and Mozart out of account; for while both are supremely accurate and complete masters of counterpoint, Purcell is notoriously unable to construct on a large scale, and Mozart is as schematic in the perfection of his large forms as in his details.

Be this as it may, invertibility is an ancient and important accidental quality of melody. Some theorists have even ascribed to it the origin of the minor mode both in melody and in harmony. Such theories are beyond the scope of the present discussion, and indeed they concern a more accurate kind of inversion than has ever been contemplated by composers.

Two points concern us here: first, that not all melodies will invert with good results; and secondly, that an inversion is accurate enough if it corresponds to the original by degrees of its scale regardless of semitones. There is no ingenuity in inverting a melody; you have only to turn the page upside down and read the result in a looking-glass to correct it from turning backwards as well. But, as Walford Davies shows in his decisive summary of the subject of *Invertible Counterpoint* in Grove's Dictionary, the process, applied to the second subject of Beethoven's Violin Concerto, will have a hideous result. In two fugues of W. K. Bach inverts a theme with crude results, a tautology in I. 8, and a harshness in I. 20. Both these cases seem to me decidedly beyond the limit of a protecting privilege without which no work of art could have freedom to grow; the privilege by which a theme too artificial to appear as an original statement may be acceptable as a variation. The inversions in Contrapunctus XI seem to me to lie well within this privilege; the mirror-fugues sometimes suggest the need for it; while in the final version of the augmented canon the bass of bars 14–25, paraded aloft in the treble of 66–77, behaves as if it merely meant to annoy. Technical difficulties certainly do not explain this; as Appendix B proves, if proof were needed. However, though we have long outgrown the notion that Bach was a mere calculator of musical mathematics, we need not swing round to the opposite paradox and maintain that not even in K. d. F. is Bach capable of pursuing a problem beyond its purely musical sphere of interest. But the difficulty with this augmented canon, and the other canons, lies in finding what the problem can be. I incline more and more to the inference that Bach has not stated the problem; that these canons go relatively no further than Beethoven's Promethean *Introduzione col Basso del Tema*,[1] and that Bach prefers to make his augmented canon as grotesque as possible, not only because he can thus be recklessly inventive with its leader, but because he has as Lamb-like a pleasure in a bad joke as Beethoven at bars 9–12 of his *Basso del Tema*. Perhaps we may conclude that Bach himself would admit that if he could not do better with extended canon by augmentation than he has done here, in *Das Musikalische Opfer* and in the variations on *Vom Himmel hoch*, the problem is unprofitable. Cancrizans (i.e. backwards) canon he probably regarded as a mere joke: there is a good epigrammatic one in *Das Musikalische Opfer*; but I do not imagine Bach wasting time over a longer one.

Evidently the problem of total harmonic inversion, though at first sight more abstruse still, is not unprofitable. On the contrary, the emergency that seems almost to have taken Bach by surprise in Contrapunctus XI is one that might have turned up at any time in his career. His many inverted themes often occur in simultaneous pairs; as when a fugue with an invertible subject has an invertible counter-subject (*see* W. K., I. 15, II. 22). It is the merest accident that, as far as I know, he never had occasion to invert the themes of a whole phrase of triple counterpoint until he wrote Contrapunctus XI. If my view of the course of events here is correct, he took for granted that his triple

[1] Variations, Op. 35, on a theme from *Die Geschöpfe des Prometheus*.

combination would invert until he found that it would not. Then he devised the method that permanently solves this problem.

Cherubini carries the problem a step further. He devotes a chapter of his treatise on counterpoint to the device he calls 'inverse contrary imitation'; which he illustrates by a passage which, with some alterations and considerable development, actually occurs in his monumental Credo for double chorus. The passage is very smooth, and nobody would notice anything remarkable about it. But the two choirs imitate each other by mirror-inversion in a major scale $\left\{ \begin{array}{l} \text{EDCBAGFE} \\ \text{CDEFGABC} \end{array} \right\}$ of which the converse tones and semitones correspond. This is as if the Inversus of Contrapunctus XII were designed to begin two bars after the Rectus, to continue in combination with it, and to have its tones and semitones in exact correspondence with no play of modulation at all.

Evidently, for this sort of thing Bach was too busy even when he was writing to illustrate his technique.[1]

What is the method of his mirror-fugues? Wilhelm Rust (B.-G. XXV), in denying Mizler's statement, shows us precisely what the method is not. It is the old eternal story of the hopeless squalors of Don't against the rousing stimulus of Do. Rust says that a composition like Contrapunctus XII demands renunciation in all directions, and that in particular it allows no suspensions, because in the inversion they would resolve incorrectly. This is, indeed, the point on which Bach stumbled in Contrapunctus XI; and it is true that he avoids suspensions in the mirror-fugues. But Ex. 24 shows the positive side of the question, though Bach did not live to demonstrate it. The positive rule is 'Resolve your suspensions with the kind of resolution that will work both ways'. (*See* the one faint trace of a suspension in Contrapunctus XIII, bar 34.)

As a matter of fact, the restriction is not so severe as it

[1] There is, however, a portrait of him holding a scroll on which there is a delicious little six-part canon of this kind.

sounds. With young students the difficulty is to develop any readiness to use suspensions at all; and critics would admire the suspensions of Palestrina and Lasso less if that resource were more constantly used by those masters. But you must not expect mirror-counterpoint to come by chance. It needs constant attention, from which no rule of thumb can relieve the constructor.

The study of ordinary double and triple counterpoint is seriously hindered by negative statements of the conditions of these devices. No sane musician will dispute the usefulness of art-forms without which Bach could have written no episodes but rosalias in Buxtehude's manner and Beethoven could not have developed his later style. Accordingly it is not unimportant that the rules of these things should be stated as methods and not as inhibitions.

Students who have been taught that in triple counterpoint a complete triad is inadmissible have practically been taught that all triple counterpoint is either jejune or incorrect. What they should have been taught is that in all ordinary double and multiple counterpoint 4ths and 5ths, wherever they occur, must be treated as if they were 4ths from the bass. That is the condition on which Bach is enabled to use complete harmony in all his multiple counterpoint. We shall see later that there is a ridiculously simple way of ensuring this condition. Similarly, the main rule for D. C. in the 12th is not that you must beware of the 6th, but that you must treat it like the 7th which it will eventually produce. Moreover, the special stability of the 5th should be pointed out as a feature of this counterpoint (*see* Contrapunctus XIV). Again, what is the use of telling the student that in order to produce D. C. in the 10th he must avoid all consecutive similar intervals whatever? He should be told that the contrary motion which is a virtue in all counterpoint becomes a necessity here. Lastly, it is mere nonsense even to mention these devices, as Cherubini does, without explaining their musical purport. No wonder some teachers

have dismissed them as medieval hocus-pocus. Such perkiness
is deplorable, and could not be committed by anybody who
knew the *Pleni sunt coeli* of the B minor Mass or Brahms's
Variations on a Theme of Haydn; but the blame for it lies with
Cherubini's educational methods. The perkiness of to-day
is the academicism of to-morrow; and both are thoroughly
unclassical.

How does the matter stand in regard to stretti? In the first
place Bach gives no countenance to Cherubini's view that
stretti and counter-subjects are among the 'eight essential
elements of a fugue'. From that view arises the inference, often
laid down in text-books, that 'a good fugue-subject *should be
capable* of at least one harmonious stretto'. Bach is not able to
refute this in K. d. F., because his motto theme has to be as
capable as Habakkuk. But the fact is that of all Bach's fugues
at least two-thirds have no stretto at all, nor any capacity for
stretto in their subjects; while most of the stretto-fugues have
no counter-subject. Of course, you can reconcile Bach with
Cherubini by calling every piece of imitative episode a stretto;
but this is not the way to study Bach, though it may be the way
to preserve corrupt institutions.

The lines in K. d. F. are perfectly clear; there are plain
fugues with undifferentiated episodes (I, II) and with organized
episodes (III, IV); stretto fugues, plus inversion of subject, but
without counter-subject (V, VI, VII); and fugues in the main
orders of double and triple counterpoint (VIII, IX, X, XI,
XIV) with no stretto (IX), with casual stretto-like imitations
(VIII, XI) and with any number of genuine stretti from 2 to 10.
Neither of the mirror-fugues has a stretto: if we assign that
term to the imitative treatment of the varied subject of
Contrapunctus XII, we renounce all intention of learning the
facts from Bach.

As to rules for the construction of stretti, there are none but
those of trial and error. It is a far cry from the harshness of
W. K. I. 8 and I. 20, to the smoothness of K. d. F. VI–VII,

or, for that matter, to anything else in W. K. itself. Long experience of trial and error must have gone far to make the Bach of 1750 unconscious of trial and insusceptible to error. An imposing view of the achievement of his combinations may be obtained by tabulating all their possibilities as well as their actualities; and the student, imagining that such tables were the basis of Bach's calculations, gasps at Bach's appalling industry and is deterred from prying further.

The musical facts are richer than the tabulated items, and the tabulated items reduce themselves to a few essentials. A stretto that works in one direction will probably work in a converse way; if one of these two will invert, so will the other; thus four stretti are provided by one radical combination. If the subject moves conjunctly between the lower leading note and the upper 6th of the scale, the direct and inverted forms will probably combine in a similar stretto, and we shall now have eight stretti. If a different radical combination is possible we shall have 16, far more than any one fugue could exhibit. One of the grandest and smoothest fugues in W. K. is II. 22. It develops one set of stretti, which is the closest of three equally possible sets originating respectively at 1 minim at the 7th (the set used), 2 minims at the 8ve, and a whole bar (3 minims, at the 9th. Contrapunctus X is probably one of eight possible similar fugues. How many unused possibilities there are in K. d. F. I have not the slightest idea. They will eventually all reduce themselves to the identity

$$Ex.\ 20\ a = Ex.\ 20\ a.$$

But let us put these things on their proper aesthetic (or practical) basis. Bach is evidently not worried by having to select the best combinations out of a billion possibilities thrown at his head by the arithmetical properties of the scale of D minor. His subject is not a silly thing like the notorious *Nodus Salamonis*, which was merely a way of distributing the notes of a common chord so that thousands of voices could follow the scheme without any two proceeding in consecutive unisons or octaves, with a result perfectly represented by drumming an 8-note G major chord on the pianoforte until your neighbours send for the police. I believe that the theme of K. d. F. is typically capable of two radically different stretti, each of which has four cases: by diminution it is typically capable of two more, which produce another eight; and by augmentation it can produce most of these multiplied together while the slow augmented notes occasionally stir. By this time the redoubled pence for each nail in the horse's shoe have already amounted to a few thousand pounds. But you need not think that the theme of K. d. F. will produce stretti at random: if you do not remember the actual ones, you may find them hard to guess. The incident in Contrapunctus X at bars 23–26 is a delightful example of how the obvious can prove deceptive.

Stretti are special cases of double and multiple counterpoint; which is one reason why a multitude of them can so often be reduced to one or two radical cases. Now there is a certain evasiveness about the traditional teaching of multiple counterpoint. Students who have been taught that it forbids complete common chords usually account for such forbidden fruit in Bach (and in their own efforts) by supposing that the inversions which would reveal its wickedness are not used. But it so happens that those very inversions are the only ones that are of any use at all. The whole object of the device is to provide constant change of surface and bass. Changes that concern only the inner parts are insignificant. In a triple counterpoint there are six changes, all of which are important as they all affect either bass or treble if not both. I know of no case where Bach uses all the six. There are three reasons for this: first, that five may take up quite enough room; secondly, that Bach does not think himself forbidden to repeat a combination— which leaves him with less room for the others; and thirdly, that with the sixth combination all three themes will have appeared twice in the treble and twice in the bass; so that five or six combinations do not contain appreciably more variety than three or four.

Arithmetic tells us that a quadruple counterpoint has 24 permutations; that the quintuple counterpoint in the 'Jupiter' Symphony has 120; and that the sextuple counterpoints in Bach's *Nun ist das Heil* and C major triple concerto have 720. When we have piously gasped, not only at the brains that conceived these prodigies, but at the patience that wrote out all the 720 positions and searched out those that were free from illicit 4ths, we may descend to *terra firma* and face the following facts. 1. The only positions that matter are those that change either or both the top and the bottom. 2. Those that change the top without changing the bottom are more important than those that change the bottom without changing the top. 3. Those that change both are the most important of all, and in any one composition there cannot be more of them than there are themes. 4. These changes will arise automatically if the voices take up each theme in rotation. 5. If the 5th of a chord will remain long enough (quiescent or ornamented) to acquire a dominant sense, it will certainly invert as the bass of a legitimate $\frac{6}{4}$ chord (*see* W. K., I. 4, 2nd subject). If any 5th or 4th fails to satisfy this condition it probably knows quite well that Bach or Mozart will have a free orchestral bass ready to catch it when it falls.

The truth about great music is too important for us to acquiesce in the 'spoof' that so often usurps the title of classical tradition.

The student may amuse himself by accumulating statistics of the kind so dear to the older writers of text-books, showing the order of entries of the parts. He will find Bach refreshingly indifferent towards inequalities that do not reach the ear. One really bold example in Contrapunctus VII has been pointed out in the analysis. Amongst other inequalities, the bass of VII has the subject by augmentation and diminution, but never in its normal size. On the whole the inner parts of K. d. F. have more entries of themes than the outer; a state of things found elsewhere in Bach's mature works, e.g. in the Fugue of the Chromatic Fantasia.

As to order of entries in the exposition, there is not much point in trying to impose rules upon common sense. Adjacent voices are in the normal pitch-relations for subject and answer; alternate voices (**S, T; A, B**) tend to be an octave apart and, therefore (as in Contrapunctus VI), more suited to inverted answers; in Contrapunctus VII the extreme parts **B, S** are the only ones that give room for Bach's three comic diminished answers to strut this way and that without crossing. Some distributions rule themselves out; there is no harm in the order Subject, Answer, Answer, Subject, as in W. K., I. 1; but Subject followed by three entries in the answer-position would be stupid; and fugues at the octave, though they are said to exist, are likely to be dull.

III. *Possible Groupings with Preludes.*

The whole K. d. F. as completed in the present edition could be played in a little more than an hour and a half, including Appendix C (as representing Bach's alleged intention) but not duplicating Contrapunctus XIII by treating its version for two Claviers as a separate number. Appendix C takes about ten minutes; my conclusion of Bach's unfinished fugue may be taken to be within a very few bars of the length intended by Bach; that fugue with that conclusion takes eleven minutes. Performances have been given of K. d. F. orchestrated, excluding the unfinished fugue; and the effect has proved very impressive, in spite of such drawbacks as the conception of most of the fugues as in the same tempo, and the complete irrelevance of the orchestration to the purposes either of the music or of an orchestra. Classical part-writing is harmonic draughtsmanship, and it cannot fail to sound well if played by any instruments not disqualified by compass or lack of mobility, and not manifestly incapable of making a well-balanced group. But Bach, though his orchestration is so different from that of the nineteenth century that its existence as an art has only recently been acknowledged, is as unwilling as Wagner or Bantock to regard pure four-part counterpoint as the proper food for an orchestra. Moreover, it is not by accident that the whole of K. d. F., except the mirror-fugues, lies within the grasp of two hands on one keyboard. That is a restriction which Bach will not tolerate unless it is necessary. Not for two consecutive lines (if for as much as one) will you find Bach's organ pedal parts staying within reach of the left hand, even if you take the pedal part only in the 8 ft. register. Nor in a sonata for cembalo with flute or violin will you find that the right hand can tackle the part of the other instrument as well as its own. In *Das Musikalische Opfer* the six-part fugue is one of my favourite pianoforte pieces, being strictly keyboard music; but I had rather play the end of *Götterdämmerung* from full score than tackle the quick movements of the Trio for Flute, Violin, and Continuo.

Let there be no mistake: the keyboard style of K. d. F. is a fundamental fact. There is one stretch of a 10th in Contrapunctus VIII; there is an exactly similar stretch in W. K., I. 8. There is a pedal note at the end of Contrapunctus VII that needs a little help; there is one that needs a great deal in W. K., I. 20.

A stretch of a tenth needs a large hand; and on the harpsichord, clavichord, and organ the failure to retain a stretch has a detestable effect. It is therefore significant that Bach's exceptional 10ths are in positions where the little finger of the left hand may safely let the bass go. In bar 282 of my finish to Contrapunctus XIV this is not so, though the passage is perfectly safe on the pianoforte. But I was strongly tempted to substitute a lower D for the top note of the alto: this would be the final proof of the authenticity of the passage if we did not happen to know exactly where Bach wrote his last notes. Orchestrate K. d. F. by all means; but only for the same reasons that would induce you to orchestrate W. K. If you think the task necessary you show that you understand neither orchestration nor keyboard style. If you think it artistic you must then undertake the responsibilities of idiomatic translation. Merely to transcribe, even for a string quartet, is amiable at all times, illuminating in the first result of hearing polyphony played with real ease, and childish if carried further. Mozart wrote out string-parts for four W. K. fugues; and these 'arrangements' figure among his works in Köchel's catalogue. But they do not prove that he could not play the W. K.

How are we to present K. d. F. in public as keyboard music? The first eleven numbers are by no means ineffective in their finally given order. The group of three stretti-fugues (V, VI, VII) sags dangerously; but if people have made up their minds to listen to an hour or so of Bach all in D minor and all on one theme they will be far too resigned to notice this; and Contrapunctus XI undoubtedly closes an epoch grandly. Still, I do not find that even these 45 minutes of music on one theme and in one key have anything like the unity and climax of the 45–50 minutes of the Goldberg variations. In the Goldberg canons (ranging from unison to 9th and placed in numerical order at every third variation) there is a dictionary arrangement as there is in these eleven fugues. But though every contrapuntal device, rightly used, has its character (as when Kuhnau indicates the doubts of Gideon by the argumentative harmonic style of a canon in the 2nd) there is nothing to prevent these canons from suiting their character to their surroundings. And there *is* something in a stretto-fugue by augmentation and diminution that makes it an anticlimax after a stretto-fugue by diminution alone. In any but an encyclopaedic series Bach would have seen no need to bring augmentation into all parts but would have put it into an extra pedal part at the end of an enlarged Contrapunctus VI.

After Contrapunctus XI we need more hands than two, and more keyboards than one. And no human ear will ever detect either a definite contrast or a definite relation between the Rectus and Inversus of a mirror-fugue, except the obvious inversion of the subject. Contrapunctus XIII is in itself a fugue by contrary motion before it is inverted, and the fact that its Rectus begins with the motto-theme in the inverted position is a mere accident. Except for the last bar it might be difficult to guess which was Rectus and which Inversus. Moreover, if Contrapunctus XIII were known only in the 4-part version for 2 Claviers extraordinary acumen would be needed to discover that the twin fugues had a mirror relation at all. Even with all the evidence before them, good scholars like Rust have made mistakes in sorting the free parts.

Evidently, then, the mirror-fugues are at the parting of ways between artistic contrast and dictionary sequence. No grouping of four unaccompanied two-part canons can be any better than a dictionary arrangement. The singing-master who indicates the next step in a vocal exercise by playing the chord of C and following it at once by the chord of D flat, is not more insensitive than the enthusiasts who can regard these canons as a group.

And so we come to the great torso. I confess that I use it, with my completion, as a concert piece. It needs a prelude. Except in these quasi-didactive works K. d. F. and *Das Musikalische Opfer*, the cases in which Bach has left a fugue, big or small, late or early, without a prelude are so rare as to be evidently accidental. He often seems, like Mozart in his C major Fantasia, to 'compose the prelude while writing down the fugue'; and so, if anything should interrupt him, the fugue is more likely to be left complete and stranded than the prelude. There is thus a dearth of unmarried preludes in D minor suitable for K. d. F. But there are some that are not very happily married, and Bach himself has no superstitions about transposing the key. The fugues W. K., II. 4 and II. 8 were originally in C minor and D minor respectively, and were transposed merely because he wanted representatives for C sharp minor and D sharp minor. The French Overture was composed in C minor and transposed to B minor merely to complete the set of keys represented by the other six Partitas and the Italian Concerto.

Now I have never been able to play the early D sharp minor fugue W. K., I. 8 after the sublime E flat minor prelude. The piety that accepts the crudities of that fugue will never have the presumption to understand the prelude or any other of Bach's persuasive utterances. (My beloved master Hubert Parry removed a mountain of obstruction from my view of music when he pointed this out.) Now transpose Contrapunctus III or Contrapunctus X to D sharp minor, and you will find either of them perfect companions to the E flat minor prelude. (I feel a sentimental objection to transposing the prelude.)

Again, the Clavier Toccata in D minor is an early work with a fine prelude, a wonderful interlude, and two archaic and dry quick movements chopped into Ollendorfian clauses and entitled fugues by sheer discourtesy to polyphony. One should not be in the mood for enjoying these puerilities in their juxtaposition to the apocalyptic young Bach of *Gottes Zeit*. Substitute Contrapunctus II for the common-time Presto, and follow the interlude by Contrapunctus IV as finale, and you have a Toccata in the grandest possible style with its two fugues on related themes. The difference of nearly thirty years between the two styles is philologically interesting but perfectly harmonious. Or we might select Contrapunctus IV and Contrapunctus IX as the fugues; but Bach, while he does not mind what happens after a tonic close, usually follows an introduction that ends on the dominant by a theme that begins on the dominant. However, he breaks this rule in the C minor organ fugue with the $\frac{6}{4}$ prelude.

By extending the scheme considerably beyond the bounds of

a Toccata we could work in these fugues thus without using that licence:

Toccata-introduction.
Contrapunctus IV.
Toccata-interlude.
Canon in the Octave ($_{16}^{9}$).
Contrapunctus IX.

Bach arranged the A minor violin solo sonata as a clavier sonata transposed down to D minor. In this arrangement the fugue sounds long and monotonous, giving the keyboard nothing to correspond to the business that can keep the violin strenuously occupied for 287 bars. The introductory adagio would make a fine prelude to a lively K. d. F. fugue if it did not end on the dominant, thus leaving us again with Contrapunctus IV as the only possible sequel, unless we break Bach's rule about dominant openings after dominant closes. But that rule is not absolute. (*See* the C minor organ fugue with the prelude in $_{4}^{9}$ time.)

The finale I use as a prelude to Contrapunctus XIV. The light one-part arpeggios, almost unadulterated from the original violin music, throw the four-part polyphonic into glorious relief, while the extended binary symmetry is exactly what Bach himself in 1750 would desire as a background for the vast Miltonic paragraphs of his fugue. There is no question of spoiling the sonata by such use, for nobody will ever play it as a whole in the clavier version.

Any of the canons can be used as a prelude to any of the fugues. The canons in the 8ve ($_{16}^{9}$) and 12th give no difficulty to the interpreter. I strongly recommend Appendix B in preference to the later version of the augmented canon.

The torso of Contrapunctus XIV is longer than any complete Bach fugue; and only the great so-called 'Dorian' organ fugue attains as much as two-thirds the size of the complete scheme. Yet the appearance of the motto-theme of K. d. F. in the completion, being a surprise depending its relevance to the other fugues, makes it highly desirable that this gigantic movement should not stand alone.

Here is a short half-hour with the Art of Fugue unadulterated by preludes and interludes:

Contrapunctus I.

Contrapunctus IX.

- Canon in the Octave.

Contrapunctus XIV.

Here is a good forty minutes, ending with XIV and diversified by preludes and interludes:

Adagio from D minor Sonata (transcribed violin solo).

Contrapunctus IV.

Canon in the 12th.

Andante (F major) from D minor Sonata.

Contrapunctus IX.

Finale of D minor Sonata.

Contrapunctus XIV.

I find Contrapunctus VIII too big for any group; you might as well ask for another B minor organ fugue to match the one we know. Nor is there anything to call for explanation in its use of the motto-theme, which simply enters as the third member of the triple counterpoint in an exposition as broad as the opening itself. Contrapunctus XI is a composition that not only improves on acquaintance but improves much faster when we take it on its own merits and forget the derivation of its themes from VIII. I would like to be very sure of my audience before I capped the climax of VIII by the subtleties of XI.

There are still some fine preludes waiting for use. Precedents may be found in W. K., I. 14, 20, and 23 for providing preludes quite as small as the Inventions and Sinfonias to fugues quite as important as the average of K. d. F. So why not use the D minor Invention and the D minor Sinfonia? Those in C minor and E minor would not be harmed by transposition; and of the great Four Duets that in E minor would make a splendid D minor prelude to Contrapunctus VIII. Again, we need not so confuse technique with aesthetics as to despise the 12 *Uebungen für Anfänger* (*Exercices pour les commençants*) and the 6 *Kleine Praeludien*, from which, with and without transposition, we can get another seven preludes and interludes. Slow movements may also be chosen in F major or B flat. But if you cannot make your group into a toccata-like or sonata-like scheme there is no point in doing more than provide single fugues with single preludes. The point of a toccata-like framework is that the toccata so often contains a couple of fugues on allied themes; and in *Das Musikalische Opfer* Bach shows us how to apply the notion to a sonata on the largest scale. But we cannot expect that Bach's precedents will be the only or always the best ways of dealing with an unprecedented work.

The only point on which my mind is finally made up is that the present sequence of movements in K. d. F., even as far as I–XI, is only accidentally more tolerable as a group than a straight run through half a book of W. K.; and to present it thus is to flout all sense of artistic sequence and of the greatness of such compositions as III, IV, VIII, IX, and X. It is no fairer to the rank and file, each member of which has its own urgency to become an independent piece of music, whatever educational task may have been entrusted to it by its creator.

Printed and bound in Great Britain by Hollen Street Press Ltd at Slough